If You Want Peace in This Life

Other books by Fr. Timothy M. Gallagher, O.M.V.
from EWTN Publishing:

*A Layman's Guide to the Liturgy of the Hours*

*Overcoming Spiritual Discouragement*

*Venciendo el Desanimo Espiritual*

*A Biblical Way of Praying the Mass*

Timothy M. Gallagher, O.M.V.

# If You Want Peace in This Life
## The Spiritual Letters of Venerable Bruno Lanteri

EWTN Publishing, Inc.
Irondale, Alabama

Copyright © 2025 by Timothy M. Gallagher, O.M.V.
Printed in the United States of America. All rights reserved.

Excerpts from the letters in "His Whole Being Was at Peace" are from *Begin Again*, copyright © Timothy Gallagher. Reprinted by arrangement with The Crossroad Publishing Company, www.crossroadpublishing.com.

Cover design by LUCAS Art & Design, Jenison, MI.

Cover photo courtesy of Pixabay: mountain-church-8990195_1920.jpg.

Unless otherwise noted, Scripture quotations are from the *New American Bible*, revised edition © 2010, 1991, 1986, 1970 Confraternity of Christian Doctrine, Washington, D.C. and are used by permission of the copyright owner. All Rights Reserved. No part of the New American Bible may be reproduced in any form without permission in writing from the copyright owner. Quotations noted by "RSVCE" are from the Catholic Edition of the *Revised Standard Version* of the Bible, copyright 1965, 1966 by the Division of Christian Education of the National Council of the Churches of Christ in the United States of America. Used by permission. Some Scripture quotations have been translated directly from the original French of Venerable Bruno's letters.

Excerpts from the English translation of the *Catechism of the Catholic Church* for use in the United States of America copyright © 1994, United States Catholic Conference, Inc.—Libreria Editrice Vaticana. English translation of the *Catechism of the Catholic Church: Modifications from the Editio Typica* copyright © 1997, United States Conference of Catholic Bishops—Libreria Editrice Vaticana.

No part of this book may be reproduced, stored in a retrieval system, or transmitted in any form, or by any means, electronic, mechanical, photocopying, or otherwise, without the prior written permission of the publisher, except by a reviewer, who may quote brief passages in a review.

Sophia Institute Press
Box 5284, Manchester, NH 03108
1-800-888-9344

www.SophiaInstitute.com

Sophia Institute Press® is a registered trademark of Sophia Institute.

paperback ISBN 978-1-68278-431-0

ebook ISBN 978-1-68278-432-7

Library of Congress Control Number: 2025935135

First printing

*To the priests of the Oblates of the Virgin Mary,
who introduced me to Venerable Bruno Lanteri:
those whom I knew personally, Frs. Giovanni Bonini, O.M.V.,
Vittorio Moscarelli, O.M.V., and Paolo Calliari, O.M.V.,
with the Oblate Fathers who preceded them
and made possible their work and my own*

Venerable Bruno Lanteri

*From the Decree of St. Paul VI Declaring the Heroicity of the Virtues of Venerable Bruno Lanteri:*

> His Holiness, Paul VI, having prayed earnestly, in conclusion, on this day, after celebrating Mass with great fervor, called the Most Reverend Cardinals Arcadio Maria Larraona, Prefect of the Sacred Congregation of Rites; Benedetto Aloisi Masella, Relator of the Cause; and me with them, as Secretary, and solemnly decreed that "the Servant of God, Pio Brunone Lanteri, priest and founder of the Congregation of the Oblates of the Virgin Mary, practiced the theological virtues of faith, hope, and charity toward God and neighbor, as also the cardinal virtues of prudence, justice, temperance, and fortitude, with their associated virtues, to a heroic degree."
>
> Rome, 23 November 1965
>
> Arcadio Card. M. Larraona,
> Prefect of the Sacred Congregation of Rites
>
> Ferdinando Antonelli, O.F.M., Secretary

# Contents

Acknowledgments . . . . . . . . . . . . . . . . . . . . . xi

Introduction . . . . . . . . . . . . . . . . . . . . . . . . 1

1. "You Tell Me That You Are Troubled by Temptations" . . . 5
2. "In Your Letter, I Sense Discouragement" . . . . . . . . . 15
3. "With a Holy Tenacity" . . . . . . . . . . . . . . . . . . . 23
4. "These Sacraments Are the Channel" . . . . . . . . . . . 29
5. "Loving Attention to the Inspirations of God" . . . . . . 37
6. "He Himself Descends upon the Altar" . . . . . . . . . . 45
7. "The Constant Practice of Meditation and Spiritual Reading" . . . . . . . . . . . . . . . . . . . . . . 51
8. "Say Then with Boldness, 'Now I Begin'" . . . . . . . . . 59
9. "Adhere Only to the Holy and Adorable Will of God" . . . 65
10. "Close the Door to Discouragement" . . . . . . . . . . . 69
11. "Let Us Fix Our Gaze of Faith on the Crucifix" . . . . . . 75
12. "I Thank the Lord from My Heart" . . . . . . . . . . . . 81
13. "In His Own Time He Will Set You Free" . . . . . . . . . 87

14. "An Ounce of Prayer Made with Patience" . . . . . . . . .95
15. "If You Want Peace in This Life" . . . . . . . . . . . . . . 101
16. "This Will Be the Remedy for Any Sadness" . . . . . . . 107
17. "Careful Never to Belittle Yourself" . . . . . . . . . . . . 115
18. "Paradise Pays for Everything". . . . . . . . . . . . . . . . 121
19. "His Whole Being Was at Peace" . . . . . . . . . . . . . . 125

    Prayer for the Intercession of
    Venerable Bruno Lanteri . . . . . . . . . . . . . . . . . . . . 133

    Endnotes . . . . . . . . . . . . . . . . . . . . . . . . . . . . . . . 135

    Bibliography. . . . . . . . . . . . . . . . . . . . . . . . . . . . . 139

    Sources of the Letters . . . . . . . . . . . . . . . . . . . . . . 141

    Resources . . . . . . . . . . . . . . . . . . . . . . . . . . . . . . 143

    About the Author . . . . . . . . . . . . . . . . . . . . . . . . 145

# Acknowledgments

I express my sincere gratitude to Devin Jones for his encouragement to undertake this book, to Nora Malone for her generous and competent editorial assistance with this book, and to the readers, whose comments improved its content: James Gallagher, Carol Lankford, Rachel de Almeida Oliviera, Cabrini Pak, and Elizabeth Valeri. To all, my heartfelt thanks.

# Introduction

Venerable Bruno Lanteri lived and offered spiritual direction in troubled times that included the height of the Enlightenment, the crucible of the French Revolution, the saga of the Napoleonic Empire and Wars, and the first years of the fragile Restoration. His small nation, the Kingdom of Piedmont, in what is today the northwestern corner of Italy, lay at the crossroads of these events. In his lifetime, Venerable Bruno witnessed repeated wars, prolonged French occupation with persecution of the Church, and the beginning of the Italian Risorgimento, which created the modern Italy and would end with a pope as prisoner in the Vatican. Through these years also, the cold, severe image of God that characterized Jansenist-inspired pastoral practice lay heavy on the hearts of men and women who sought to follow Christ. Echoes of all this will appear in the letters that follow.

Through it all, Venerable Bruno, "a man of a hundred tongues and a hundred arms,"[1] offered sure spiritual guidance to many people. During the French occupation, Napoleon's director of police for the region wrote to his superior in Paris, "I must inform you, Monsieur, that Monsieur l'abbé Lanteri has great influence through his hearing of confessions. He is one of the most sought after in the city,"[2] that is, Turin, the capital of the Kingdom of Piedmont.

During these tumultuous years—are they so different from our own?—with a sure hand and with a shepherd's love, Venerable Bruno guided the many men and women who sought his spiritual aid. In this book, we will watch him do so.

You desire sincerely to love and serve the Lord. You strive daily to do this. God is the center of your life. But a burden lies on your heart. It does not stop you, but it weighs upon you. You feel that you are less than the Lord would wish. You see your limitations, your failings, and the joy of your relationship with God is diminished. In the nineteen letters that follow, you will hear Venerable Bruno speak to this place in your heart.

Most of these letters are complete. For various reasons, some are not. In several cases, we have only Venerable Bruno's draft and not the final copy sent to the recipient. In these drafts, he does not give the name of the person, the place, or the date. This allowed him to keep the text without compromising the identity of the person—an important consideration in times of police surveillance and persecution. These drafts also demonstrate the seriousness with which Venerable Bruno pondered his replies to those he guided. They help explain the rich content of these letters, compact and substantial, letters that go straight to the point and offer practical guidance. Once satisfied with his text, Venerable Bruno copied the letter, adding his initial salutation and closing. When I have placed a salutation and a closing in brackets, this indicates their absence in the draft and their addition from salutations and closings in similar letters.

In one case (letter 14), we have only quotations gathered by Venerable Bruno's assistant, Father Giuseppe Loggero, from a longer letter of spiritual direction. At times, I have omitted parts of letters that repeat counsels given in others, as well as details linked to the times that would be of less interest today.[3]

Venerable Bruno knew and used three languages: Italian, French, and Latin. His letters are written in either Italian or French, depending on the recipient. Quotations from Scripture are in Latin, in keeping with contemporary usage, as are occasional theological maxims. Venerable Bruno translates the Latin as helpful for the recipient. I have rendered these letters in English with close attention to the originals and a view to readability in English.

Each recipient is an individual, with the richness of a single personality. Venerable Bruno knows how to speak to all with gentleness and clarity, always with warmth and understanding. These men and women who received his letters know that they can openly share with him their struggles, fears, and discouragement. They know that their sharing will be reverenced. To each, Venerable Bruno offers counsel with the heart and wisdom of a spiritual father.

Above all, and in every letter, his message is encouragement. Over and over, he writes, "Do not be troubled," "Be at peace," "Do not be concerned," "Be patient with yourself," and the like. The root of this encouragement is his profound sense of God's goodness, the goodness and love with which God views these sincere men and women as they struggle. As you read, you will find that he shares this same message with you.

I give these letters in chronological order. The first shows us Venerable Bruno in his thirties, the last at age seventy, one year before his death and already in his final illness. Because the letters in draft form do not provide dates, I place these according to the best date their content allows.

Above all, this is a book to be prayed. It may be simply read, and reading Venerable Bruno's wisdom and encouragement will be valuable. The book will bear the most fruit, though, when read with prayer—when read as the recipients read these letters: slowly, perhaps repeatedly, absorbing their content, taking it to heart, conversing with the Lord. To aid such reading, I introduce each letter with a brief description of the recipient, the background of the letter, and opportune comments on its content. Then, adopting Venerable Bruno's own method, I invite you to read the letter slowly, thoughtfully, prayerfully. At its conclusion, I highlight several points for further prayer.

I found the labor of creating this book inspiring and uplifting. I am happy to share it with you now. May it bring you the encouragement its content offered years ago and continues to offer today.

# 1

## "You Tell Me That You Are Troubled by Temptations"

Venerable Bruno writes to a woman burdened by temptations and afraid that she is not responding well. Is she alone in this?

She seeks to live a good Christian life, but her conscience is delicate and close to scruples. What were her temptations? Venerable Bruno tells her that "it would be easy to be kind when it costs nothing, patient when our patience is never tried, and chaste when there is no struggle." In all likelihood, such are her temptations.

He reassures her repeatedly: "Do not be troubled"—almost a refrain in this letter—"dismiss every doubt," "always keep your soul in peace," "do not blame yourself for this," and similar exhortations. He offers a wealth of practical counsels toward this end.

We have only Venerable Bruno's draft of this letter and so not the name of the addressee. It is a young Bruno who writes, in his late twenties or thirties, no older than thirty-nine. At that age, the Father Diessbach who asked him to guide this woman died, concluding a holy and fruitful priesthood.

Venerable Bruno cites Scripture repeatedly in this letter and twice refers to Saint Francis de Sales, whose writings and spirit he deeply assimilated. The root of Bruno's counsel is his profound consciousness of God's goodness—hence the confidence to which he calls this woman, and us.

Read, now, this letter. Read it as Venerable Bruno himself desired to read spiritual texts, "with lively faith, hope, and love ... stopping for a moment where the words speak to you, with desire, with pauses, with the affection of your heart, and with reflection."[4]

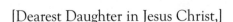

[Dearest Daughter in Jesus Christ,]

As our beloved Father Diessbach has asked me to assist you spiritually, I believe that I would fail in this responsibility if I did not do so to the best of my ability, with reflection and prayer. I know my own insufficiency, but the thought that I did not seek this role and that it was given to me by my superior, and therefore by God, consoles me. And so I trust that God will help us both, and I pray for this every morning when I celebrate Mass, knowing that prayer is the surest means for obtaining from God the

## "You Tell Me That You Are Troubled by Temptations"

blessings and graces that we need and that he gives without limit to those who ask him.

You tell me that you are troubled by temptations. Take care, in the first place, not to consider this something bad. Rather, be sure that we must undergo temptations. God wills this so that we might have opportunities to practice the different virtues and not grow careless in the spiritual life. Scripture teaches this clearly. The life of man, Job says, is a continual battle [Job 7:1], and Sirach says: my son, when you enter God's service, prepare your soul for temptation [Sir. 2:1]. It was because you were acceptable to God, Saint Raphael says to Tobit, that it was necessary for you to be tried by temptation [Tob. 12:13].[5] Saint Paul, after he was raised to the third heaven, had to suffer a thorn in the flesh so that his virtue might be further purified [2 Cor. 12:1-9].

More than all this, the Holy One of all holy ones, Jesus Christ, also willed to undergo temptations [Matt. 4:1-11]. Thus, we should consider temptations as favors and be filled with spiritual joy according to Saint James's teaching, when he says: my brothers, consider that all joy in this life consists in bearing temptations, knowing that in temptation we exercise patience and, with patience, all virtue [James 1:2-3]. In fact, it would be easy to be kind when it costs nothing, patient when our patience is never tried, and chaste when there is no struggle. Be sure, then, that temptations are a good that God permits, and be confident, as our Faith teaches, that he will never allow you to be tempted beyond your strength [1 Cor. 10:13].

Second, you must learn to go forward even in your failings, and be certain that you will commit many because only in Heaven can we serve God without these. Saint Francis de Sales says that perfection does not consist in never falling but in rising immediately, knowing our weakness, asking God's forgiveness, but with peace of heart and without surprise, telling God that we have acted according to what we are, and may he act according to what he is. We need to learn, when we fall, to rise at once, asking forgiveness, never tiring of rising again, though we fall a thousand times. If a child would not rise again and walk because he falls often or out of fear of falling at every step, he would never learn to walk.

We need, then, to grasp the greatness of God's goodness and not measure it by our limitations, thinking that he tires of our inconstancy, weakness, lukewarmness, and forgetfulness and so, because of our sins, withdraws his help and denies his grace. Such misunderstanding of God makes it difficult to ask his forgiveness when we fail in our spiritual practices. Our good God is not so. God has no need of us except to show us mercy. Let us attribute to him what is truly characteristic of him—that is, his goodness, mercy, and compassion, that he is a loving Father who raises us when we fall, who never tires of forgiving us, to whom, on the contrary, we give great joy and honor when we approach him to ask his forgiveness.

Third, resolve never to do deliberately anything that you know will displease God, and, having resolved this, do not be troubled by temptations or by anything that may be evil in itself, as long as you are not aware of them. As soon as you do become aware of them, pay no attention to them but, rather, consider them and make use of them as a stimulus to make an act of love of God, of trust, of repentance for sin, and the like. Even if these temptations should last all day, do not be troubled, as there is no evil in this. This is not in your control; let them come and go, and tell God that you want none of this, and that you will bear this as long as he wills. Simply face this with patience, with freedom of spirit, and with peace of heart.

When the temptation has passed, never examine whether you consented but turn your attention to something else. If you are not able to do this and scruples arise as to whether you gave consent, then either you doubt only as to whether you consented, and, in that case, disregard this, dismiss every doubt, make this sacrifice of mind and will, and obey Father Diessbach; or you are certain that you gave consent, in which case, peacefully renounce this before God, unite yourself with God, knowing your weakness, rejecting the temptation, and ask forgiveness, sure beyond doubt that God gives it; or you recognize that there was some negligence in your response, some defect, and you remember that only in Heaven will we serve God without defects, and you humble yourself, and this leads you to greater confidence in God.

Therefore, both in time of temptation and after, always keep your soul in peace, with freedom of heart. In this way, you will serve God more fully and with joy.

I would say the same about the intensity you experience when you do things. Do not be troubled by this. God permits you to experience this so that you can exercise patience. And so, do not be troubled by this as long as you are not aware of it. As soon as you do become aware of excess, do not be troubled. Try to moderate what may be excessive, and even if there should still be some defect in this, do not be surprised, as you are not yet an angel.

Even with these counsels, at times you will feel a burden to yourself and without desire for these things. Do not blame yourself for this. It is because God is asking you to carry the cross, which is the way to Heaven. Saint Teresa of Ávila says this. And it is good to hear Saint Paul, who carried his cross and said that we need to be patient with ourselves [1 Thess. 5:14]. In patience, you will possess your souls [Luke 21:19]. However you find yourself, do your

## "You Tell Me That You Are Troubled by Temptations"

usual spiritual practices as well as you can, always with complete confidence in the goodness of God. Learn to go forward even with your failings, and serve God whether with good or bad dispositions, because these are not of our choosing.

For the rest, be sure that when you persevere in your desire to please God, even should you fall into some defect or failing, God does not cease to love you because of this. God, our good Father, has compassion on us because he knows of what we are made.

Be of good heart, then, seek always to be joyful, and entrust yourself as much as you can to God. Dismiss any doubt; always tell him that you never want consciously to offend him. Do not be troubled. God is with you, and he is helping you. He will not let you fall. Read chapters 9 and 10 of *The Introduction to the Devout Life*.[6]

[Pray for me, and I am your servant in Jesus Christ,
Father Bruno Lanteri]

---

Take time now to reflect and pray with the following:

1. "Consider it all joy, my brothers, when you encounter various trials, for you know that the testing of your faith produces perseverance" (James 1:2-3).

Joy, various trials, testing of your faith, a testing that produces perseverance: ponder the meaning of this.

You experience this testing, too, in the circumstances of your life. Speak to the Lord about this, about your various trials. Pray for that perseverance. Pray for that joy.

2. "We need to learn, when we fall, to rise at once, asking forgiveness, never tiring of rising again, though we fall a thousand times. If a child would not rise again and walk because he falls often or out of fear of falling at every step, he would never learn to walk."

Never tire of rising again, though you fall a thousand times—"*never* tiring." Ask for this grace.

3. "Let us attribute to him what is truly characteristic of him—that is, his goodness, mercy, and compassion, that he is a loving Father who raises us when we have fallen, who never tires of forgiving us, to whom, on the contrary, we give great joy and honor when we approach him to ask his forgiveness."

"What is truly characteristic of him." Ponder this slowly: goodness, mercy, compassion, a loving Father, great joy and honor when we ask forgiveness. Pause here. Do not hurry by this. Ask for the grace to *know* this.

4. "Even with these counsels, at times you will feel a burden to yourself and without desire for these things. Do not blame yourself for this. It is because God is asking you to carry the cross, which is the way to Heaven."

## "You Tell Me That You Are Troubled by Temptations"

You feel a burden to yourself, you feel a lack of desire for spiritual things. Do not blame yourself. God is asking you to carry the cross, "which is the way to Heaven."

5. "Be of good heart, then, seek always to be joyful, and entrust yourself as much as you can to God. Dismiss any doubt; always tell him that you never want consciously to offend him. Do not be troubled. God is with you, and he is helping you. He will not let you fall."

Yes, be of good heart! Seek always to be joyful. Dismiss any doubt. God is with you. He will not let you fall.

2

# "In Your Letter, I Sense Discouragement"

At the age of twenty-seven, Leopoldo Ricasoli began spiritual direction with Venerable Bruno, a direction that ended only with Venerable Bruno's death twenty-five years later. The two met on several occasions, but because of the distance between them—Venerable Bruno lived in Turin, and Leopoldo, in Florence—the greater part of this direction occurred by letter. Forty-eight letters of their correspondence have been conserved. That Leopoldo saved these letters indicates the value he placed on them.

Leopoldo was intelligent, well-educated, upright, warm, and well-mannered. He loved music and art. The deep center of his life was his faith, and he took part in every initiative involving the Church in his native Florence. At eighteen, he married Lucrezia Rinuccini, and together they had seven children—four sons and three daughters. Two of their sons became priests. Sorrow entered Leopoldo's life when his beloved wife died at forty-eight. Two of his sons also died young, the first leaving behind three children, and the second, four. Leopoldo died at the age of seventy-two.

Notwithstanding his authentic Christian life, Leopoldo frequently fell prey to discouragement in spiritual matters. In a letter to Venerable Bruno written at age forty-eight, he expresses this affliction:

> I ask you once again from the heart to remember me often before the Lord when you celebrate Mass, that he grant me true sorrow for my serious sins, which are most grave, the grace of final perseverance, and the grace to provide in the best way for the education of my young Stanislao, who is about to turn twelve.

And in the same letter:

> I have great need of overcoming sloth and lukewarmness in God's service. I have great need of growing more fervent and acquiring a little zeal for the salvation of my neighbor, and of overcoming my accursed human respect and the grave temptations that I suffer against the faith. I place my woes candidly before you that you may help me quickly by your prayers and gain for me also the help of the prayers of many good persons whom you know. I know that I ought rather to pray myself for my needs, but I repeat that I am lazy and waste time without praying, or by praying lukewarmly.[7]

Venerable Bruno will urge Leopoldo again and again and with energy to resist discouragement. The remedy he proposes

## "In Your Letter, I Sense Discouragement"

is well-centered and accessible: fidelity to the sacraments and to the daily practices of the spiritual life.

When Leopoldo mentions his "serious sins, which are most grave," to what does he refer? Neither he nor Venerable Bruno specify further, and Leopoldo's goodness of life was universally recognized. One possibility is that he means "the grave temptations that I suffer against the faith" described here and which greatly burdened his heart, causing him to fear for his eternal salvation. If so, this is both a sign of Leopoldo's sensitive spirit and of the Jansenist-tinged pastoral practice that burdened the hearts of good people.

Venerable Bruno is forty-five and writes in a time of intense apostolic activity. His use of the words "Friend" and "Christian Friend" in the salutation and closing refer to their common belonging to the Christian Friendship, a group dedicated to the interests of the Church.[8] Certainly, it also describes the deep bond between the two. Venerable Bruno's words in the following letter regarding "the great goodness you showed me" refer to Leopoldo's hospitality during Venerable Bruno's trip to Florence the preceding year. His encouragement of "more than weekly Holy Communion" was remarkable in a day when only yearly Communion, if that, was common.

Leopoldo is the spiritual brother of all who sincerely follow Christ and are prone to discouragement. Is that not all of us, at least at times—perhaps often? Venerable Bruno is the spiritual father of us all when we, too, love Christ and yet experience such discouragement.

Here, as in all his spiritual letters, Venerable Bruno leads with the heart, with "true and heartfelt joy" at the opportunity to assist one whose spiritual well-being is so important to him.

Read, now, this letter. Read like Venerable Bruno, "with lively faith, hope, and love ... stopping for a moment where the words speak to you, with desire, with pauses, with the affection of your heart, and with reflection."

Monsieur and dear Friend in Jesus Christ,

I do not want this mail coach to depart without writing you a short note in haste. I usually wait for the day the coach leaves to write, and usually some unforeseen occupation impedes me from writing as I planned. That is what happened last week, and that is what is happening again today.

 I cannot hide the true and heartfelt joy that your esteemed and welcome letter gave me. I awaited it with impatience, and I hope you will renew this gladness for me weekly if you can, all the more because this is not just a question of satisfying my wish and my concern in your regard, which certainly are not small, because I can never forget the great goodness you showed me, but this is a question of God's glory, which can be promoted by this means; and so, do not refuse me this joy.

## "In Your Letter, I Sense Discouragement"

In your letter, I sense discouragement in the service of God. For God's sake, guard against this because there is no enemy more to be feared than this. A holy tenacity in the faithful practice of your ordinary spiritual exercises, especially in meditation and spiritual reading, will always be a source of great blessings for you. Add to this a weekly practice of the Sacrament of Penance and more than weekly Holy Communion, with a firm and invincible resolution always to begin again and to hope ever more firmly in God, and I guarantee you safety from major failings, at least from their unhappy consequences, which you fear with such reason. It is of these matters especially that I beg you to write and tell me how you find yourself, because the well-being of your soul, which certainly cannot be indifferent to me, depends principally on these.

I have no more time to write. I beg you to present my respects to Madame the Marquise, your worthy spouse. Be assured that I will never forget you in my prayers before God. As I wait to hear once more from you, I recommend myself to your prayers, and I am in haste,

Your Servant and Christian Friend,<br>
Fr. Bruno Lanteri<br>
Turin, February 29, 1804

## If You Want Peace in This Life

Take time now to reflect and pray with the following:

1. "This is a question of God's glory, which can be promoted by this means."

God's glory: all that serves to make God more known and loved in human hearts in this life and for eternity. How is God calling you to "promote" that glory?

2. "In your letter, I sense discouragement in the service of God. For God's sake, guard against this because there is no enemy more to be feared than this."

Do you experience "discouragement in the service of God"? Venerable Bruno urges, with the strongest language he knows, that is, "for God's sake," to guard against this. Such discouragement is the greatest enemy "to be feared" in the spiritual life. Ask now of the Lord the grace to guard against this.

3. "A holy tenacity in the faithful practice of your ordinary spiritual exercises, especially in meditation and spiritual reading, will always be a source of great blessings for you."

The remedy is readily at hand: "a holy tenacity," a daily fidelity, to your ordinary practices of the spiritual life. Two such practices: daily meditation and daily spiritual reading. This tenacity "will always be a source of great blessings for you." Speak now to the Lord about these practices in your life. Ask for this tenacity, this daily fidelity.

4. "Add to this a weekly practice of the Sacrament of Penance and more than weekly Holy Communion, with a firm and invincible resolution always to begin again and to hope ever more firmly in God, and I guarantee you safety from major failings."

A blessed guarantee—one that promises eternal salvation!

Five benefits of regular Confession: it helps us to "form our conscience," "fight against evil tendencies," "let ourselves be healed by Christ," "progress in the spiritual life," and, by it, "we are spurred to be merciful as he is merciful" (*Catechism of the Catholic Church* [CCC], no. 1458).

"The Church strongly encourages the faithful to receive the Holy Eucharist on Sundays and feast days, or more often still, even daily" (CCC 1389). Strongly.

Speak now with the Lord about both of these sacraments in your life.

5. "A firm and invincible resolution always to begin again and to hope ever more firmly in God."

"Firm": unwavering. "Invincible": unable to be overcome. "Always": without fail. Our response to any failing: every time, a new beginning, with stronger hope in God. Ponder this response to your failings. Ask it of the Lord.

# 3

# "With a Holy Tenacity"

A further letter to Leopoldo Ricasoli, ten months after the preceding. Leopoldo continues to worry about grave sin and the state of his soul. Venerable Bruno delights in "the special graces" God has bestowed upon Leopoldo and strongly counsels Leopoldo against discouragement. Once more, he offers him a sure remedy: frequent reception of the sacraments and fidelity to his daily spiritual practices.

Now read this letter. Again, read like Venerable Bruno, "with lively faith, hope, and love ... stopping for a moment where the words speak to you, with desire, with pauses, with the affection of your heart, and with reflection."

# If You Want Peace in This Life

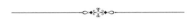

Turin, November 28, 1804

Monsieur and very dear Christian Friend in Jesus Christ,

Your letter consoled me greatly, as I had been unhappy not to have heard from you for so long! I thank you sincerely because, by writing, you have lifted no small worry from my heart. Forgive me now if my reply comes later than I would have wished, as I had hardly received your letter when some special business took all my time.

May the Lord be eternally blessed for the special graces he has willed to bestow on you. Oh! If only we could truly understand how precious the state of grace is, what sacrifices would we not make and what victories over self would we not be prepared to undertake to conserve this state. For this reason, I can never recommend too highly to you daily meditation on the holy teachings of our Faith, made with true dedication and devotion and pursued with a holy tenacity and always, as much as possible, at the same time of day.

Spiritual reading done unhurriedly, every day, from well-chosen spiritual books will assist you greatly in carrying out this exercise.

You will all the more surely remain in the state of God's grace if you do not neglect to approach the holy sacraments weekly and even more frequently, if necessary. These are the channels through which the Lord chooses especially to share with us his graces, which above all we need.

I rejoice greatly and thank God from my heart to find you with such dispositions and with such firm resolutions, nor do I allow a single day to pass without holding you particularly present at the altar, praying that the Lord grant you holy perseverance.

Above all, I beg you with all my might to keep yourself from discouragement, trouble of heart, and sadness, and so, seek constantly to calm your poor heart and encourage it and to serve God always with holy joy; and let your resolutions always be these two, which I counsel you to renew frequently with holy tenacity: first, never to offend God knowingly, and second, should you commit some failing, never to persevere in this with your will but immediately to lift yourself with humility and courage and to begin again, firmly convinced that God forgives you the moment you ask his forgiveness with humility and trust.

I do not doubt that the Lord God, who has already given you such special graces, will continue to bless you, to enable you to serve ever more his greater glory.

I close by rejoicing from my heart with you and your most worthy wife on the happy birth of a son [Alessandro]. Please give her my regards, being assured that I will always keep them both present in my poor prayers, nor will I cease to ask for them every blessing from Heaven. With heartfelt sentiments of esteem and consideration, I am

> Your humble and devoted Servant
> and Christian Friend,
> Father Bruno Lanteri

---

Take time now to reflect and pray with the following:

1. "May the Lord be eternally blessed for the special graces he has willed to bestow on you."

> Pause now. Think back over your life and recent times. See the "special graces" that God has bestowed on you. Let your heart express gratitude to God.
>
> Saint Thérèse of Lisieux to her sister Céline: "Gratitude is the thing that most draws upon us the graces of our good God, because if we thank him for one blessing, he is touched and hastens to send us ten more, and if we thank him again with the same gratitude, he multiplies his graces beyond calculating! I have experienced this. Try it, and you will see."[9] Yes, try it. Try it now. For what can you express gratitude to God?

2. "Oh! If only we could truly understand how precious the state of grace is, what sacrifices would we not make and what victories over self would we not be prepared to undertake to conserve this state."

## "With a Holy Tenacity"

"Sanctifying grace is a habitual gift, a stable and supernatural disposition that perfects the soul itself to enable it to live with God, to act by his love" (CCC 2000). Reread the following sentence slowly, attentively, and ponder each phrase: "Oh! If only we could understand how precious the state of grace is."

3. "I can never recommend too highly to you daily meditation on the holy teachings of our Faith, made with true dedication and devotion, and pursued with a holy tenacity and always, as much as possible, at the same time of day."

Daily meditation through reflection on biblical passages, imaginative contemplation of them, through *lectio divina*; parts of the *Liturgy of the Hours*, the Rosary, with digital helps, and so forth. The means are many. Venerable Bruno says, "I can never recommend too highly to you daily meditation on the holy teachings of our Faith." Meditation on the truths of our Faith. Daily. Speak with the Lord about this.

4. "Spiritual reading done unhurriedly, every day, from well-chosen spiritual books will assist you greatly in carrying out this exercise."

Spiritual reading: a book, a podcast, a talk on YouTube, or the like. Daily. Five minutes? Ten? Fifteen? While commuting to work? While your hands are busy but your mind is free? This practice, Venerable Bruno says, "will assist you greatly."

5. "Above all, I beg you with all my might to keep yourself from discouragement, trouble of heart, and sadness, and so, seek constantly to calm your poor heart and encourage it and to serve God always with holy joy."

Again and again, and with all his energy: "Keep yourself from discouragement, trouble of heart, and sadness," and "seek constantly to calm your poor heart and encourage it and to serve God always with holy joy." Seek this grace. Ask for it now. Ask the Lord to show you the path out of discouragement and into holy joy.

# 4

## "These Sacraments Are the Channel"

Venerable Bruno traces here a spiritual program for a married woman. He gives no date, but he most likely wrote this text in his forties, possibly a little earlier. The name of the woman also is not mentioned. From the text, it appears that she received her education at a monastery and lives a faithful spiritual life. She is now married. No mention is made of children, which may indicate a marriage of recent date.

Venerable Bruno writes in the person of this woman: through her words, he speaks. What follows is part of this lengthy text, sections that reveal characteristic traits of Venerable Bruno's spiritual direction and that apply universally.

Read this text. Read like Venerable Bruno, "with lively faith, hope, and love ... stopping for a moment where the words speak to you, with desire, with pauses, with the affection of your heart, and with reflection."

# If You Want Peace in This Life

May Jesus Live

*Spiritual Guidelines That Will Lead to Stable Happiness for Me, My Husband, and the Whole Family*

I am created by God for this sole purpose, that is, to praise and serve him and, in the end, be saved for eternity; nor am I asked to praise and serve him in any state but in that state to which he has called me. Like a candle, I must burn and be consumed for God, but where he wills and in the way he desires.

*Some Particular Means to Help Me Do This*

I will go to Confession and receive Communion every eight days, as I have done for years. These sacraments are the channels that God has established to pour out upon me his graces and inspirations. My perseverance, therefore, depends on my constancy in approaching these sacraments. When I receive Confession and Communion, I will ask the Lord in a special way to fulfill the responsibilities of my state of life, especially to love and be loved by my husband and to please him in all that is not a matter of sin.

Every day, I will be faithful to fifteen minutes of meditation and fifteen minutes of spiritual reading and to the examination of conscience in the

## "These Sacraments Are the Channel"

evening, and I will assist at Mass if I can. Devotion must be nourished, or it weakens, and there is nothing more to fear than lack of reflection. I have the whole day for my activities; it is right that I give an hour to God when the duties of my state of life permit.

I will try to mortify myself in little things, in leaving certain words unsaid, in not needing to see everything. I will let no day pass without some victory over my emotions, whether denying myself something that I want or bearing difficult things with a gentle spirit. I will call to mind how much Jesus Christ did for my salvation, and I will find courage for these actions in the thought that the One who gave everything, merits everything. I will exercise mortification especially in rising on time in the morning in order to fulfill well the duties of my state of life and have time for my spiritual practices.

I will always profess a special and tender devotion to the Sacred Heart of Jesus and to the Virgin Mary, which are the source of all graces. I will turn to them in time of need that they may grant me the light and grace I need, firmly convinced that it is impossible for them to abandon me and not be active on my behalf.

I will also have great devotion to Saint Teresa of Ávila and to my guardian angel.

Practicing all these spiritual means faithfully, I am sure to fulfill well the duties of my state of life, and I will experience the peace of heart that God gives to those who serve him and that the world cannot give.

Into whatever failings I may fall, I will never lose heart, knowing that I will commit many of these, but I will immediately ask God's forgiveness, and I will always seek to do better. If I should fall even a thousand times a day, a thousand times I desire to begin again, knowing more clearly my weakness, and with unshaken peace of heart, I will promise God to do better. I will take care not to think of his Divine Majesty as though he were of our condition, that he grows weary of such wavering, weakness, and forgetfulness, and so responds by removing his help and the graces we need. Such thoughts are the foolishness of our ignorance, and we do God a great wrong when we think this way, measuring him by our own limitations. Rather, I will always attribute to him what truly corresponds to him and what he regards most highly—that is, his goodness, mercy, and compassion, to be a loving Father who knows our weakness, who bears with us and forgives us, knowing that discouragement is the greatest obstacle on the way of salvation.

Generosity of spirit, freedom of heart in acting and in suffering, fidelity to resolutions made to God, peace, joy, love of neighbor, compassion for the sufferings of others, goodness, patience, forbearance, a warm heart, acquiescence in all that does not offend God — in short, to be gentle and humble of heart [Matt. 11:29]: this is the character I desire to have and that I will constantly ask of the Sacred Heart of Jesus and of Mary.

Take time now to reflect and pray with the following:

1. "I am created by God for this sole purpose, that is, to praise and serve him and, in the end, be saved for eternity."

"Created by God." "For this sole purpose." "To praise and serve him" by my life. "And in the end, be saved." Eternal salvation, eternal life with God — this is the ultimate goal of my life. Ponder these fundamental truths. Speak to the Lord about them.

2. "Every day, I will be faithful to fifteen minutes of meditation and fifteen minutes of spiritual reading and to the examination of conscience in the evening, and I will assist at Mass if I can."

Each day, fifteen minutes of some form of meditative prayer in the way that best helps you, fifteen minutes of spiritual nourishment through reading or listening, the examination of conscience in the evening, daily Mass and Communion when possible. Could you do this? At least part of it? What would happen if you did? Speak to the Lord about it.

3. "I will try to mortify myself in little things, in leaving certain words unsaid, in not needing to see everything. I will let no day pass without some victory over my emotions, whether denying myself something that I want or bearing difficult things with a gentle spirit."

"Leaving certain words unsaid," "not needing to see everything," "some victory over my emotions" daily, "denying myself something," "bearing difficult things with a gentle spirit." What would happen in your life and to your household if you lived this way daily?

Read and meditate on 1 Corinthians 13:4-7: "Love is patient, love is kind.... It is not quick-tempered...."

4. "If I should fall even a thousand times a day, a thousand times I desire to begin again, knowing more clearly my weakness, and with unshaken peace of heart, I will promise God to do better."

You wanted to do better in that area, but you fell. You fell again . . . and again. "If I should fall *even a thousand times a day*, a thousand times I desire to begin again." And do this, yes, with clearer knowledge of your need for God but also with unshaken peace of heart. Tell the Lord sincerely that you want to improve. And do this every time you fall.

5. "I will take care not to think of his Divine Majesty as though he were of our condition, that he grows weary of such wavering, weakness, and forgetfulness, and so responds by removing his help and the graces we need."

## "These Sacraments Are the Channel"

We tire of others' forgetfulness, tardiness, indecision, and so on, and we think God acts like this toward us. Never, says Venerable Bruno, think of God this way. "Rather, I will always attribute to him what truly corresponds to him and what he regards most highly—that is, his goodness, mercy, and compassion, to be a loving Father who knows our weakness, who bears with us and forgives us." To see God this way, according to truth, lifts the heart. Pause to ponder on this.

# 5

## "Loving Attention to the Inspirations of God"

Sister Leopolda Mortigliengo was born in Turin and entered the Visitation Sisters in that city at age seventeen. After thirty-nine years in the monastery, she, along with many other women religious, was evicted from her convent by the French police, who sought the suppression of religious life. Sister Leopolda returned to her family, and a difficult time began for her. For the next fourteen years, until her death, she struggled to maintain what she could of her religious life while living at home. Through these troubled years, she sought the spiritual guidance of Venerable Bruno. Twenty-four of his letters to her have been conserved.

Sister Leopolda, like so many others, brought her failings and discouragement to Venerable Bruno, whose understanding, counsel, and encouragement fortified her through these demanding years. One letter from her to Venerable Bruno has been conserved, and citations from it will provide insight into her spiritual struggles. She has just made, as best she could in the family home, an eight-day retreat and now writes to Venerable Bruno.

Evidently, Venerable Bruno counseled her to base her retreat on the book *Meditations* written by Jesuit Father Claude Judde, an author with whom Venerable Bruno was familiar. The Father Luigi Guala to whom Leopolda refers was a disciple of Venerable Bruno who, living in Turin, was able to accompany her during those eight days. Venerable Bruno could not do so because of his exile from Turin by order of the French police, ultimately Napoleon, in view of Venerable Bruno's actions on behalf of Pope Pius VII, whom Napoleon held captive at this time.

Leopolda writes:

> I found the rereading of *Meditations* of Father Judde very helpful, without, however, adding any thoughts of my own, consistently finding myself too dull and unable to generate a good thought. I saw that my faults are always the same. I regret that until now I have let my prayer go; and even as I reproach myself for my infidelity, I am unable to resolve to undertake it. During all the eight days of the retreat, it was only by seeking the help of books that I was able to complete the times of prayer.
>
> I have kept all the duties of my religious life very badly during this past year. I spent this whole year doing myself continual violence to conquer myself and adapt to the way of living in our household, but

all without merit, for I did it only because I had no choice and without purity of intention. It seems to me that I hear you say that we must always, and in every moment, begin again, and this will be my third resolution, but it is very hard to see myself always beginning without ever finding any improvement.

Father Guala was good enough to help me as much as the Lord made possible. I told him that I am always troubled by daily Communion because I see that I do not profit from it and only go out of habit, that I go almost without preparation. I suggested that I should go twice a week and on all feast days, as our [Visitation monastic] rule says, but he did not wish to consent to this without your approval.[10]

"Dull and unable to generate a good thought"; "my faults are always the same"; "I have kept all the duties of my religious life very badly during this past year"; "it is very hard to see myself always beginning without ever finding any improvement": this is a good woman, whose life is dedicated to God, who finds herself in difficult circumstances, who feels her spiritual poverty, and who struggles. Is there any one of us who cannot nod in agreement, who does not feel something of this, and who does not desire help and encouragement?

In the letter that follows, Venerable Bruno discusses Leopolda's annual retreat, for which, this year also, she has asked his help. His reference to his physical issues reflects the harsh conditions of his exile and their repercussions on his ever-fragile health. Once again, he encourages, "Be patient with yourself," "Remain in peace," "Do not let yourself be disturbed."

Read, now, Venerable Bruno's letter. Read "with lively faith, hope, and love … stopping for a moment where the words speak to you, with desire, with pauses, with the affection of your heart, and with reflection."

---

To the Honorable Sister Leopolda Mortigliengo
February 23, 1812

Dear Sister and daughter in Jesus Christ,

I was very happy to receive your letter, which was welcome to me. As regards your retreat, the time is not yet opportune. I am not sure if it will be possible during Lent; most likely it will have to be after Lent.

    I am happy to learn that you experience many good and holy desires. Be sure that none will be left without its reward. If you give constant and loving attention to the inspirations of God throughout the day, he will multiply these inspirations, and you will be well recompensed for your times of dryness in meditation.

    With regard to your interior struggles and the empty thoughts you find in yourself, be patient with

## "Loving Attention to the Inspirations of God"

yourself and remain in peace; give these little weight. Bear with them as if they were noisy persons quarrelling in the streets outside. And if you find the courage for this as well, humble yourself before God and thank him for these humiliations that begin to make you more like him. Say to him, "It was good for me to be afflicted, in order to learn your statutes" [Ps. 119:71]. Do all this in your heart; as regards your interactions with others, express your reasons with peace and gentleness, and do not let yourself be disturbed.

Regarding my own retreat, I am still very much behind. I do it in the midst of illness, as you see, and thus I will barely finish it during Lent.

Pray very much for me. I bless you,<br>Father Bruno Lanteri

Take time now to reflect and pray with the following:

1. "I am happy to learn that you experience many good and holy desires."

If you are reading this, it is because God has blessed you, too, like Leopolda, with "many good and holy desires." Your faith is important to you. You desire to grow spiritually. Let your heart be glad over the work of God's grace in you.

2. "If you give constant and loving attention to the inspirations of God throughout the day, he will multiply these inspirations."

Yes, give "constant and loving attention" to God's inspirations. Loving attention. What are these inspirations in your life now?

3. "Be patient with yourself."

"Patience attains all things" (St. Teresa of Ávila).[11]

"Love is patient" (1 Cor. 13:4).

"Remember that holiness is not attained in twenty-four hours" (Venerable Bruno).[12]

And so "be patient with yourself."

4. "Say to him, 'It was good for me to be afflicted, in order to learn your statutes' [Ps. 119:71]."

Yes, these "interior struggles," these "empty thoughts" are burdensome, but God is working for your growth and progress even through these. From such affliction comes a blessed learning.

Thus, "remain in peace; give these little weight"; "bear with them as if they were noisy persons quarrelling in the streets outside," an unwelcome disturbance but nothing more.

5. "As regards your interactions with others, express your reasons with peace and gentleness, and do not let yourself be disturbed."

*"Loving Attention to the Inspirations of God"*

Share your thoughts, your views, your needs "with peace and gentleness" when you speak with others.

"The fruit of the Spirit is ... peace, kindness, generosity ... gentleness, self-control" (Gal. 5:22). Ask for this Spirit.

# 6

# "He Himself Descends upon the Altar"

In this text, Venerable Bruno outlines a program of spiritual life for another woman, not identified in the draft conserved. The date, too, is uncertain. We read here Venerable Bruno's thoughts on the Mass with his original and lovely way of praying the Mass from the heart. He likewise details how to profit from spiritual reading. The reference to reading harmful books reflects his times, when the printed word was the chief vehicle of transmitting ideas — in contrast with today's Internet, television, and associated channels of communication.

Read, now, Venerable Bruno's text. Read "with lively faith, hope, and love ... stopping for a moment where the words speak to you, with desire, with pauses, with the affection of your heart, and with reflection."

## Regarding the Mass

To miss Mass without reason is to lack faith or zeal for our salvation. To be convinced of this, it is enough to remember that the Sacrifice of the Mass is the renewal on the altar of the same sacrifice of Jesus Christ on Calvary. He himself descends upon the altar at the words of the priest and offers himself for the same purpose as on Calvary. The fruit of the Mass is so great that one Mass alone would be enough to save the world. It is in this sacrifice that Christ pours out his infinite merits in a special way.

Because the Mass is the greatest action of our religion and the one from which we can draw the greatest fruit, we must assist at Mass in the way that both the holiness of the action and our own interest enjoin: we must bring suitable dispositions to it; we must endeavor to share the sentiments of the Blessed Virgin Mary, of the Beloved Disciple, of Mary Magdalene, who were present at Calvary, to have the same sentiments that would have filled our hearts had we been present ourselves at Calvary.

*A way of attending Mass.* And to do this the more fruitfully, at the Penitential Rite we could share the sentiments of the tax collector [Luke 18:9–14]; at the "Glory to God in the highest," those of the angels at the birth of Christ [Luke 2:9–14]; at the

## "He Himself Descends upon the Altar"

prayers [Collect, Prayer over the Offerings, Prayer after Communion], the sentiments of the Church's priest, who prays for us; at the readings and the Gospel, the sentiments of a disciple of Jesus Christ, who listens humbly and desires to put his teachings into practice; at the Profession of Faith, the sentiments of the martyrs; at the Preparation of the Gifts, we can unite ourselves with the Church in offering to the eternal Father, with the Church, the sacrifice of his Son in adoration, thanksgiving, and reparation, and to ask for the graces we need; at the Preface and the "Holy, holy, holy," the sentiments of the seraphim, who praise and love God through all eternity; at the Consecration, we can adore Jesus Christ with living faith and reflect on his Passion; at the Our Father, the sentiments of a poor mendicant; at the Lamb of God, those of a wrongdoer in need of forgiveness; at the "Lord, I am not worthy," those of the humble centurion [Matt. 8:8]; at Communion, those of Zacchaeus, rejoicing to receive Jesus into his home [Luke 19:5-6]; after Communion, those of Mary Magdalene, who stayed at the feet of Jesus to weep and to love him [Luke 7:38, 47]; at the "Go forth, the Mass is ended," those of an apostle—that is, of a soul filled with fervor.

### Regarding Spiritual Reading

Nothing is more harmful than the reading of harmful books. Reading is the food of the soul, and just as we take care to choose the right food for the body, a similar care and proper order must be observed in choosing the right food for the soul.

*A way of doing spiritual reading.* Once you have chosen a book and decided how much time you can give to it, begin the reading by raising your heart to God. Reflect that it is God who speaks to you through this book, that it is a letter he sends you from Heaven; ask him for an attentive and docile heart and for the grace to understand well the truths contained in the book, to profit from them. Then, read with attention and without haste. Pause on the truths that most speak to your needs, apply these truths to your life, and lift your heart to God. Never finish the reading without some holy resolution you can practice.

Take time now to reflect and pray with the following:

1. "The fruit of the Mass is so great that one Mass alone would be enough to save the world. It is in this sacrifice that Christ pours out his infinite merits in a special way."

"One Mass." "Enough to save the world." In this sacrifice, "Christ pours out his infinite merits in a special way." What place does the Mass have in your life? What place might it have?

## "He Himself Descends upon the Altar"

2. "We must endeavor to share the sentiments of the Blessed Virgin Mary, of the Beloved Disciple, of Mary Magdalene, who were present at Calvary, to have the same sentiments that would have filled our hearts had we been present ourselves at Calvary."

- ❖ To be at Mass with the sentiments that filled the hearts of Mary, John, and Mary Magdalene.
- ❖ To be at Mass with the sentiments that would have filled your heart had you been physically present on Calvary, like them.

See the scene of Calvary. Be there. Then see Mary. See John. See Mary Magdalene. Ask for a part, at least, of their sentiments when you are at Mass.

3. "*A way of attending Mass.*"

Read this paragraph again, slowly, pausing on each part of the Mass Venerable Bruno mentions, feeling the sentiments, the heart, of the biblical figures named:

- ❖ The tax collector who humbly expresses sorrow for his sin
- ❖ The angels who rejoice at the birth of the Savior
- ❖ The disciple who listens avidly to Jesus' words and desires to live by them
- ❖ The martyrs, the centurion, Zacchaeus, Mary Magdalene ...

Let their sentiments and their hearts reveal to you a way of attending, of praying, of living the Mass.

4. "Reading is the food of the soul."

Reading spiritual books, listening to spiritual podcasts or talks on the Internet, watching Catholic television or conferences on the Internet—all this is the "food of the soul."

Bodies cannot live, cannot prosper, without food. Nor can souls. What spiritual food, what nourishment, would be right for your soul?

5. "Read with attention and without haste. Pause on the truths that most speak to your needs, apply these truths to your life, and lift your heart to God."

Read, listen, view, "with attention and without haste." Pause. Apply. Lift your heart to God. Your life of faith will deepen and grow.

# 7

## "The Constant Practice of Meditation and Spiritual Reading"

Venerable Bruno replies to a letter from Leopoldo Ricasoli, now thirty-four years old, married for seventeen years. His care for Leopoldo's spiritual well-being is evident, as is his ongoing effort to help him overcome discouragement. The remedy remains the same: fidelity to the sacraments and to the daily practices of the spiritual life—a clear and attainable path out of anxiety.

A poignant note emerges in this letter, written in Venerable Bruno's time of exile, now in its second year, "where I have become as though useless to my neighbor." At the same time, exile has become "my cherished solitude," a time of great spiritual growth, even to mystical prayer, that prepared the remainder of Venerable Bruno's life and mission. That, however, is hidden from him, and his physical ills convince him that his life will not be long: ills that "hasten my departure from this unhappy world and the union with my gentle Jesus for which I long."

In fact, Venerable Bruno's exile would endure two more years. These would be followed by twelve more years of life, the time of his most lasting works.

As in earlier letters, "Friend" and "Christian Friend" refer to membership in the Christian Friendship organization, in which the only bonds were those of friendship in Jesus. Leopoldo's title "Prior" indicates his role in a local group of the Knights of Saint Stephen.

Read, now, Venerable Bruno's letter. Read "with lively faith, hope, and love … stopping for a moment where the words speak to you, with desire, with pauses, with the affection of your heart, and with reflection."

My Worthy Signor Prior and Christian Friend in Jesus Christ,

Your letter meant much to me, and it could not have consoled me more. For a long time now, I have been especially concerned about you before the Lord and have greatly desired to learn how you were. Now may the Lord, who willed to share this with me through your letter, be praised, and may he be the more praised and blessed because I see that this news is good in every respect.

## "The Constant Practice of Meditation and Spiritual Reading"

I also see, however, that you fear for your constancy, and certainly not entirely without reason as regards yourself, because we can never sufficiently fear and even despair of ourselves and, for this reason, must all the more flee occasions and dangers. Yet, lest this fear, so just in itself, descend into discouragement and heaviness of spirit, we must inseparably accompany it with the firmest hope in God, our most loving heavenly Father. He alone can and truly desires to help us, and he infallibly does help us if we are constant in using the saving means his Father's heart provides us with for this purpose. These means are a faithful reception of the sacraments, never letting anything impede this, together with the constant practice of meditation and spiritual reading and the frequent exercise of some external mortification.

You know this is not so difficult, and a means that can help you remain firm in doing this would be to share with me, from time to time, an account in some detail of both the practice and the fruits of these exercises. In this way, I would have the consolation of contributing as much as I am able to your spiritual progress.

Do me this favor, my dearly beloved Signor Prior, so that, in this, my cherished solitude, where I have become as though useless to my neighbor, I may at least be of some spiritual assistance to you. I ask this even more because my days will not be long because of my illnesses, which, rather than diminish, persist all the more, hastening my departure from this unhappy world, and the union with my gentle Jesus for which I long. Regarding your children whom I love tenderly, rest assured that I will never forget them before the Lord. I have a firm hope that the Lord will always bless them and will give you the light you need to preserve them from the corruption of the age.

I beg you to give my special regards to your worthy spouse and to the Friends, to whose prayers I particularly recommend myself. With the greatest esteem and warm friendship and gratitude, I am,

> Your most Devoted, Indebted, and
> Affectionate Servant and Friend,
> Father Bruno Lanteri

Take time now to reflect and pray with the following:

1. "Fear for your constancy" and "firmest hope in God."

A repeated counsel of Venerable Bruno, taken from a spiritual classic he loved, Lorenzo Scupoli's *The Spiritual Combat*: the pairing of distrust of self (*diffidenza di noi stessi*) and great confidence in God (*confidenza in Dio*).

❖ A salutary distrust of our own spiritual strength, which renders us careful to "flee occasions and dangers" but which never leads to discouragement because it is inseparably linked to "the firmest hope in God, our most loving heavenly Father."

❖ The firmest hope in God. Firmest. Our most loving heavenly Father. Most loving. Think about this. Ask for these graces.

2. "He alone can and truly desires to help us, and he infallibly does help us if we are constant in using the saving means his Father's heart provides us with for this purpose."

Our loving heavenly Father can help us, desires to help us, and he infallibly—a lovely word here: this help will *never* fail us—does help us, if only we are faithful to the practices of the spiritual life.

And this is not hard, it is well within our grasp: a constancy that is itself made possible by God's grace and love.

3. "These means are a faithful reception of the sacraments, never letting anything impede this, together with the constant practice of meditation and spiritual reading and the frequent exercise of some external mortification."

Regular Confession and Mass with Holy Communion; daily meditation and spiritual reading—elsewhere, as we have seen, Venerable Bruno proposes fifteen minutes for each—and some form of self-denial for God.

These means are readily available to us all, and they lead *infallibly* to the outpouring of God's grace.

4. "A means that can help you remain firm in doing this would be to share with me, from time to time, an account in some detail of both the practice and the fruits of these exercises. In this way, I would have the consolation of contributing as much as I am able to your spiritual progress."

To be accompanied in our spiritual lives, not to be alone on the spiritual journey, to be able to share, to speak about our spiritual experience, to have "some form of dialogue" in the spiritual life (Pope Benedict XVI).[13] This is a means "that can help you remain firm."

Do you have this? A spiritual guide? A confessor? A spouse? A friend? A parish group? This is all the more important in a time when the culture does not support our life of faith.

Pray about this. How might you find "some form of dialogue"?

5. "The union with my gentle Jesus for which I long."

Eternal life. Heaven. Eternal blessedness with God, with the saints, with loved ones.

Saint Louis Martin, father of Saint Thérèse: his daughters "would often hear him murmuring in the Belvedere [his place of prayer], '*Ego ero merces tua magna nimis*' — 'I am thy reward exceedingly great' (Gn 15:1)."[14] Often.

Father Diessbach, Venerable Bruno's saintly spiritual director for twenty years: "Paradise pays for everything."[15]

*"The Constant Practice of Meditation and Spiritual Reading"*

St. Ignatius of Loyola: "Man is created to praise, reverence, and serve God our Lord, and by this means to save his soul."[16] Ask for this longing. Live for this eternal goal.

# 8

## "Say Then with Boldness, 'Now I Begin'"

Venerable Bruno writes to Sister Leopolda Mortigliengo eleven months after the preceding letter cited (letter 5), as the new year begins. She feels the burden of eviction from her monastery after almost forty years and the difficulty of living religious life as best she can in her family household. With the strongest possible language, Venerable Bruno confronts her discouragement as she looks back: "Your affliction with regard to the past has no basis; it is simply a temptation of the enemy. I can assure you of this in the name of God." Simultaneously, he urges her to have hope for the coming year.

In this letter, Venerable Bruno speaks to us all when we are burdened by our inadequacies and failures, calling us to confidence in God as we face the future.

Read, now, Venerable Bruno's letter. Read it "with lively faith, hope, and love … stopping for a moment where the words speak to you, with desire, with pauses, with the affection of your heart, and with reflection."

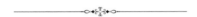

To the Honorable Sister Leopolda Mortigliengo
January 10, 1813

Dear Sister and daughter in Jesus Christ,

Your affliction with regard to the past has no basis; it is simply a temptation of the enemy. I can assure you of this in the name of God. Instead of giving in to this, therefore, give glory to God and thank him from your heart for the infinite goodness with which he has forgiven everything. This same enemy does not stop at attacking you in regard to the past; he seeks to attack you with respect to the future as well. Be watchful of this. If you did not make all the progress you wished in the past year, such will not be the case this year if you humble yourself and have all the greater hope in God, asking him without ceasing to grant you these two graces that we need so much and that he so desires to give you, having promised this to you and merited it for you.

Say then with boldness, "Now I begin," and go forward constantly in God's service. Do not look

## "Say Then with Boldness, 'Now I Begin'"

back so often because one who looks back cannot run. And do not be content to begin only for this year. Begin every day, because it is for every day, even for every hour of the day, that the Lord taught us to say in the Our Father, "Forgive us our trespasses" and "Give us this day our daily bread."

Do you not yet see that the enemy seeks in this way to strip you of your peace and confidence in God, two dispositions we so need in order to pray well? Follow, therefore, the counsel of Saint Teresa, "Let nothing disturb you," not even your own spiritual failings, because these are the object and the foundation of the infinite mercy of God, which infinitely surpasses the malice of all the sins of the world. Firmly resolved never to let yourself be troubled by anything in the world, present yourself humbly and with full confidence to the Lord in prayer, and he will not fail to have compassion on you.

Do not be concerned if prayer does not go as you would wish; it is enough that it be as God wishes. And this is not difficult; you need only avoid voluntary negligence.

Ask, then, from your heart forgiveness of the Infant Jesus for any times in the past when you lacked courage; these are only failures to grasp the infinite goodness of his Heart. And begin every day to place yourself, just as you are, in the adorable Heart of

God, which showed itself so visibly loving for sinners, not for the just.

Pray for me, and I bless you,

Your father in Jesus Christ,<br>Father Bruno Lanteri

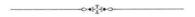

Take time now to reflect and pray with the following:

1. "Say then with boldness, 'Now I begin,' and go forward constantly in God's service."

Say this today. Say it now, and without hesitation. Say it with boldness, boldness because you know that God's love and grace are with you in this new beginning.

2. "Do not look back so often because one who looks back cannot run."

No, do not look back so often. Leave the past to God's mercy—the most blessed place to leave it. Know of his love, his closeness, and his help in the present, and walk, even run, forward with him.

3. "Begin every day, because it is for every day, even for every hour of the day, that the Lord taught us to say in the Our Father, 'Forgive us our trespasses' and 'Give us this day our daily bread.'"

A woman read these words and said: "If the day was going badly, I thought I had to wait until the next day

## "Say Then with Boldness, 'Now I Begin'"

to make a new start. Now I realize that I need not wait, that I can start again at any hour, at any moment of the day." Yes, at any hour of the day. Now.

4. "Follow, therefore, the counsel of Saint Teresa: 'Let nothing disturb you,' not even your own spiritual failings, because these are the object and the foundation of the infinite mercy of God."

Not even your own spiritual failings, because these are the object of God's infinite mercy. Spiritual failings met with infinite mercy. Pause here. Pray with this.

5. "Do not be concerned if prayer does not go as you would wish; it is enough that it be as God wishes. And this is not difficult; you need only avoid voluntary negligence."

Simply do your best in prayer, and be at peace. "You need only avoid voluntary negligence." The rest is in God's hands.

## 9

# "Adhere Only to the Holy and Adorable Will of God"

A few weeks later, Venerable Bruno again writes to Sister Leopolda. She is sixty-six, elderly for the times, with accompanying physical ills. Venerable Bruno continues to encourage her, this time to bear with the ills of age. He invites her to see God at work in allowing these and to reverence her humanity and its struggles, knowing that God accepts her goodwill in the midst of them.

Venerable Bruno's exile persists, and the occasion for the letter is the trip of his assistant, Father Loggero, to Turin, where Sister Leopolda resides. The Sister Crocifissa to whom Venerable Bruno refers is another religious evicted from her convent, whom Venerable Bruno also assists (see letter 14).

Read, now, Venerable Bruno's letter. Read "with lively faith, hope, and love ... stopping for a moment where the words

## If You Want Peace in This Life

speak to you, with desire, with pauses, with the affection of your heart, and with reflection."

To the Honorable Sister Leopolda Mortigliengo
February 6, 1813

Dear Sister and daughter in Jesus Christ,

I am taking the occasion of Father Loggero's trip to Turin to send you this brief note.

Do not be surprised at your lack of energy, listlessness, and boredom in spiritual things; this is caused by age and physical issues. God does not exempt you from these because, ultimately, it is he himself who procures them for you, and he would be asking something impossible of you. He asks only that you be patient with yourself, that you always begin with a holy tenacity to be faithful in your spiritual practices. It is enough for him that you approve in your heart what those books say, and he accepts that approval just as if you had expressed those sentiments from the bottom of your heart. You must, therefore, be content with this as well. Otherwise, we are not seeking to please God but rather to please ourselves. On the contrary, we should always seek above all what God wants rather than what we want, to have no hope in ourselves but rather in God, to adhere only to the holy and

## "Adhere Only to the Holy and Adorable Will of God"

adorable will of God, and to hope only in his infinite mercy.

This is what I wished to say to you. For the rest, I am happy that you get along well with Sister Crocifissa. Through the practice of true Christian charity, you will gain perseverance in this charity and a reward in Heaven.

Continue to pray for me, and often. I leave you in the Heart of Jesus,

Your father in Jesus Christ,<br>Father Bruno Lanteri

---

Take time now to reflect and pray with the following:

1. "Do not be surprised at your lack of energy, listlessness, and boredom in spiritual things; this is caused by age and physical issues. God does not exempt you from these because, ultimately, it is he himself who procures them for you, and he would be asking something impossible of you."

When physical issues burden your prayer, do not be surprised or troubled by this. God permits this and so does not ask that you not feel a lack of energy and listlessness in prayer.

2. "He asks only that you be patient with yourself, that you always begin with a holy tenacity to be faithful in your spiritual practices."

"He asks only that you be patient with yourself"—patient with yourself when these physical issues make prayer more difficult. Only be faithful to prayer "with a holy tenacity," as best you can, in the real circumstances.

3. "It is enough for him that you approve in your heart what those books say, and he accepts that approval just as if you had expressed those sentiments from the bottom of your heart."

You read or listen to beautiful spiritual thoughts, but physical issues make it difficult to feel them in your heart, to feel that you personally express them to God. "It is enough for him that you approve in your heart what those books say." A consoling truth.

4. "You must, therefore, be content with this as well. Otherwise, we are not seeking to please God but rather to please ourselves."

Therefore, be at peace when you experience similar struggles. God is asking you to pray in these circumstances. When you do what you can, he is pleased—he loves this effort, this acceptance, this yes to what he permits.

5. "We should seek above all ... to adhere only to the holy and adorable will of God and to hope only in his infinite mercy."

Our one desire: "the holy and adorable will of God."
Our one hope: "his infinite mercy."

## 10

# "Close the Door to Discouragement"

Sister Leopolda Mortigliengo has just made her annual retreat. In this letter, nine months after the preceding one, Venerable Bruno responds to her account of the retreat. He rejoices in its fruit, approves her resolutions, and, as always, urges her to avoid discouragement.

Following Venerable Bruno's counsel, Sister Leopolda received Communion daily, an unusual practice at the time. In her account of the retreat, however, she wrote, "I am always troubled by daily Communion because I see that I do not profit from it and only go out of habit, that I go almost without preparation" (see letter 5, introduction). She had suggested to Father Guala, who assisted her in the retreat, that she receive Communion on feast days and otherwise only twice a week. Father Guala referred her to Venerable Bruno, who answers in this letter: *on occasion*, you may omit Communion *once* a week, *if* Father Guala gives you permission—a lovely way of advising her to continue with daily Communion.

Venerable Bruno speaks of Saint Francis de Sales as Sister Leopolda's "holy father," that is, the founder of the Visitation Sisters, to which she belonged and whose spirit she strove to live in her changed circumstances.

Read, now, Venerable Bruno's letter. Read "with lively faith, hope, and love … stopping for a moment where the words speak to you, with desire, with pauses, with the affection of your heart, and with reflection."

December 19, 1813

My honored Sister in Jesus Christ,

I rejoice, and I thank the Lord from my heart that you were able to make your spiritual retreat without external distractions and in peace, as this is a great grace from the good God. I approve very strongly your three resolutions: first, purity of intention will unite you all the more to God and will also spare you many sorrows that ordinarily come from seeking oneself and not God; a holy tenacity, in the second place, in never omitting even a little of your daily prayer and your other spiritual practices will discourage the enemy from increasing the difficulty of doing them with the purpose of leading you to omit some of them; and third, the decision always

## "Close the Door to Discouragement"

to begin will close the door to discouragement, and that of itself will free you from tepidity and from past faults.

As regards Holy Communion, I give you permission on occasion to omit it once a week, if Father Guala gives you permission. When you trouble yourself about not having good thoughts when you receive Holy Communion and in your other spiritual practices, you run the risk of having the Lord keep you in that condition, because the Lord wishes that we learn well that of ourselves we cannot have any good thoughts, and this is the teaching of our Faith. When, therefore, you trouble yourself about this, it is a sign that you are not sufficiently convinced of this truth. You will say to me that you always fear that you are the cause of this, and I will not reprove you for this. But note that only a voluntarily chosen cause can harm us, and even that voluntarily chosen cause, once we dismiss it, no longer harms us because that very dismissal is of merit for us.

If you like the little book of Saint Francis de Sales and if it is a help to you, all the better. It is a sure sign that your holy father cares for you, and you should thank him for this.

I am sorry to hear of your problems with your eyes and hope they will not last. Take care to avoid the cold, which can harm them.

## If You Want Peace in This Life

I thank you that you always keep me in your prayers before God, and I certainly do not fail to do the same for you. I bless you. May God be with you.

Your father in Jesus Christ,
Father Bruno Lanteri

---

Take time now to reflect and pray with the following:

1. "Purity of intention will unite you all the more to God and will also spare you many sorrows."

Marie Guérin writes of her cousin Saint Thérèse of Lisieux: "Hers is not an extraordinary sanctity; there is no love of extraordinary penances, no, only love of God. People in the world can imitate her sanctity, for she has only tried to do everything through love and to accept all little contradictions, all little sacrifices that come at each moment as coming from God's hand. She saw God in everything, and she carried out all her actions as perfectly as possible."[17]

"People in the world can imitate her sanctity." "She has only tried to do everything through love." "Purity of intention will unite you all the more to God."

2. "Never omitting even a little of your daily prayer and your other spiritual practices will discourage the enemy from increasing the difficulty of doing them, with the purpose of leading you to omit some of them."

> Again, a holy tenacity, fidelity to our daily prayer, even when difficult. A wonderful consequence of such fidelity: "this will discourage the enemy." Yes, this is the discouragement to be sought!

3. "The decision always to begin will close the door to discouragement, and that of itself will free you from tepidity and from past faults."

> Saint Francis of Assisi, in his last years: "'Let us begin, brothers, to serve the Lord, for up to now we have made little or no progress.' ... And persevering untiringly in his purpose of attaining holy *newness of life*, he hoped always to make a beginning."[18]
>
> Saint Francis de Sales, in a letter of spiritual direction: "Be patient with all, but especially with yourself, that is, do not be troubled at all by your imperfections and always have the courage to rise again from them. I am very happy that you begin again every day. There is no better way to complete the spiritual life than to begin again every day."[19]
>
> St. Ignatius of Antioch, age seventy-three, on his way to Rome and martyrdom: "I am now beginning to be a disciple."[20] "The decision always to begin will close the door to discouragement."

4. "As regards Holy Communion, I give you permission on occasion to omit it once a week, if Father Guala gives you permission."

A gentle way of saying: receive Communion frequently, even daily, if you can.

Vatican II: the Holy Eucharist is "the source and summit of the whole Christian life."[21]

St. John Paul II: "The Holy Eucharist contains the Church's entire spiritual wealth: Christ himself, our Passover and our living Bread."[22]

What place can the Eucharist have in your life?

5. "You will say to me that you always fear that you are the cause of this [distraction], and I will not reprove you for this. But note that only a voluntarily chosen cause can harm us, and even that voluntarily chosen cause, once we dismiss it, no longer harms us because that very dismissal is for us of merit."

Distractions in receiving Communion and in prayer: harmful only if voluntary, and even then you can profit—when you dismiss them, you gain in merit before God.

# 11

# "Let Us Fix Our Gaze of Faith on the Crucifix"

Venerable Bruno writes to Sister Leopolda one month later and responds to her New Year's wishes with encouragement for the coming year. He addresses the question of suffering, to which neither was foreign, both exiled from their habitual circumstances and both bearing physical ills. Venerable Bruno invites her — and us in our various sufferings — to "fix our gaze of faith on the crucifix," to look upon the sufferings of Christ, our model and our strength.

Read, now, Venerable Bruno's letter. Read "with lively faith, hope, and love ... stopping for a moment where the words speak to you, with desire, with pauses, with the affection of your heart, and with reflection."

# If You Want Peace in This Life

January 18, 1814

My honored Sister in Jesus Christ,

I thank you from my heart for your wishes for this year expressed to the Lord on my behalf. I have not failed to do the same for you at the altar. For the rest, do not let yourself be discouraged, not even a little. Be sure that your proposals regarding your spiritual practices will not be without effect and will gain for you many graces in this year. Suffer only in seeing the defects of your soul, but rather than be disappointed, seek always to encourage your soul to begin, but *gently*, as your holy father, who loves to see us practice gentleness not only toward others but also toward ourselves, prescribed for you.

Let us also fix our gaze of faith on the crucifix, and we will find that [our Lord] was not satisfied only with the possibility of suffering but wished truly to suffer every kind of pain in body and in spirit, because it is not the mere possibility of suffering but suffering itself that brings us merit. Let us, then, accept from his hand every occasion of suffering and of practicing virtue. And because everything is disposed for our salvation, let us seek to enter his loving purpose and to adhere to it as best we can,

*"Let Us Fix Our Gaze of Faith on the Crucifix"*

sure that, with every event and with every cross, he gives his grace, and that each grace to which we adhere will have its eternal reward.

Do not forget me, I beg you, in your prayers. May God be with you.

Your father in Jesus Christ,<br>Father Bruno Lanteri

---

Take time now to reflect and pray with the following:

1. "Suffer only in seeing the defects of your soul, but rather than be disappointed, seek always to encourage your soul to begin, but *gently*, as your holy father [Saint Francis de Sales], who loves to see us practice gentleness not only toward others but also toward ourselves, prescribed for you.

> Saint Francis de Sales: "Believe me, Philothea, as the chiding of a father, made gently and with love, does much more to correct a child than irritation and anger, so also, when our heart has committed some fault, if we censure it with gentle and peaceful reproach, with more compassion toward it than passion against it, and encourage it to do better for the future, it will feel a deeper regret that will penetrate more completely than if one were to correct it with harshness, scolding, and impatience."[23]

"Seek always to encourage your soul, but *gently*."

2. "Let us also fix our gaze of faith on the crucifix."

Saint Bonaventure writes of Saint Francis of Assisi and his companions, "Christ's cross was their book, and they studied it day and night."[24]

Pope Francis: "Let us gaze upon Jesus on the cross and say to him: 'Lord, how much you love me! How precious I am to you!' "[25] "Let us also fix our gaze of faith on the crucifix."

3. "And we will find that [our Lord] was not satisfied only with the possibility of suffering but wished truly to suffer every kind of pain in body and in spirit, because it is not the mere possibility of suffering but suffering itself that brings us merit."

From the writings of Saint Rose of Lima: "Let everyone know that grace comes after tribulation. Let them know that without the burden of afflictions it is impossible to reach the height of grace. Let them know that the gifts of grace increase as the struggles increase."[26]

4. "Let us, then, accept from his hand every occasion of suffering and of practicing virtue."

In your life, you have occasions of suffering, situations that call for patience, enduring, giving, and so on. Think of these, and ask for the grace to accept these "from his hand."

5. "And because everything is disposed for our salvation, let us seek to enter his loving purpose and to adhere to it as best we can, sure that, with every event and with every cross,

## "Let Us Fix Our Gaze of Faith on the Crucifix"

he gives his grace, and that each grace to which we adhere will have its eternal reward."

"Everything is disposed for our salvation." "Let us seek to enter his loving purpose and to adhere to it as best we can." Ask for the grace to enter and to adhere. Know that "with every cross, he gives his grace" and "that each grace to which we adhere will have its eternal reward."

## 12

## "I Thank the Lord from My Heart"

This letter was written ten months later and is directed to Leopoldo Ricasoli. In it, Venerable Bruno delights in the peace Leopoldo has experienced for some time. He finds its cause in Leopoldo's regular practice of Confession and Mass with Holy Communion.

He encourages Leopoldo once again to the daily practice of meditation and spiritual reading, which will, he says, further strengthen the grace of the sacraments. In this letter, Venerable Bruno mentions specific books that may serve both for meditation and for spiritual reading. The books he lists and the ease with which he cites them give insight into Venerable Bruno's extensive knowledge of books and his wisdom in choosing the right title for each person.

Father Vincent Huby, S.J. (1608-1693), published, among other titles, *The Retreat on the Love of God and of Our Lord Jesus Christ*. Father Nicholas Roissard wrote *The Consolation of the Christian, or Reasons for Confidence in God in the*

# If You Want Peace in This Life

*Different Circumstances of Life.* Various teachings of Father Louis Bourdaloue, S.J. (1632–1704), were gathered in *The Thoughts of Father Bourdaloue of the Company of Jesus on Different Topics of Religion and Morals.* Capuchin Father Fidèle de Pau authored the volumes of *The Heart of the Christian* in the mid-1700s. All these were written in French, a language in which Leopoldo was fluent. The consoling nature of these books and their suitability for Leopoldo are evident.

Read, now, Venerable Bruno's letter. Read "with lively faith, hope, and love … stopping for a moment where the words speak to you, with desire, with pauses, with the affection of your heart, and with reflection."

Most Worthy Signor Prior and Christian Friend,

I rejoice from my heart at the peace of heart I perceive you have experienced for some time now, and you could not have chosen a better means to preserve it than the frequent practice of the sacraments. Faithfully add to this a little meditation and spiritual reading every day, and have no fear that the Lord will not grant you the other things you desire. Rest assured that the difficulty in persevering in all this consists more in misgivings than in reality. Consider that God merits every effort we can make and does not let himself be outdone in generosity.

## "I Thank the Lord from My Heart"

A book that might serve for meditation could be Father Huby's, and for spiritual reading, *The Consolation of the Christian* or *The Thoughts of Bourdaloue*, or *The Heart of the Christian*, especially the second volume, even if you have already read and reread all of these.

In any case, if you can let me know briefly about all of this, be sure that you could do nothing more welcome to me. I accept already with very great gladness your proposal of writing monthly.

Until then, I beg you to extend my warmest greetings to your worthy wife and to our common friends, and with special esteem and gratitude, I am,

> Your devoted Servant and Christian Friend,
> Father Bruno Lanteri

---

Take time now to reflect and pray with the following:

1. "I rejoice from my heart at the peace of heart I perceive you have experienced for some time now, and you could not have chosen a better means to preserve it than the frequent practice of the sacraments."

> Frequent approach to the sacraments of the Eucharist and Confession and the experience of peace. "You could not have chosen a better means to preserve it."
> Venerable Bruno again calls us to the heart of the spiritual life: the encounter with Jesus in the sacraments.

2. "Faithfully add to this a little meditation and spiritual reading every day, and have no fear that the Lord will not grant you the other things you desire."

Daily meditation and daily spiritual reading, listening, or viewing. This will strengthen your peace, diminish fear, and open you to further grace. Speak with the Lord about this.

3. "Rest assured that the difficulty in persevering in all this consists more in misgivings than in reality."

You feel the attraction of such practice of the sacraments, meditation, and reading—but your heart doubts: Is this really possible? For me? "Rest assured that the difficulty in persevering in all this consists more in misgivings than in reality."

4. "Consider that God merits every effort we can make and does not let himself be outdone in generosity."

Yes, consider this. Reflect on this—on the One who has loved you from eternity and given you life, who has redeemed you with such love, who opens to you the way to eternal life, who merits every effort we can make. And the One who will not be outdone in generosity.

5. "A book that might serve for meditation ... and for spiritual reading."

What book, what podcast, what video conference might serve for these two spiritual practices? Think about this.

Ask the Holy Spirit's guidance. Take concrete steps to find suitable resources. Make a choice. Begin.

## 13

## "In His Own Time He Will Set You Free"

In this letter, Venerable Bruno responds to a woman troubled by the attraction toward her of a man in her circle, to whose interest she herself is not indifferent. The draft conserved does not specify her state in life, but judging from its content, she is most likely married.[27] She is a woman of faith, serious about her Christian life, desirous of full fidelity to her commitments before God, and with her own spiritual struggles as well. She cannot avoid all contact with this man because of his proximity, and consequently, she is disturbed. Unsure of how to act, she has asked Venerable Bruno for counsel. In this letter, he replies with his customary clarity and encouragement: God is permitting this trial to help her grow in other important ways as well; his grace, always with her, is infinitely more powerful than any temptation; she should be gentle toward herself and others as she bears this trial.

# If You Want Peace in This Life

❁ ❁ ❁

Read, now, Venerable Bruno's letter. Read "with lively faith, hope, and love ... stopping for a moment where the words speak to you, with desire, with pauses, with the affection of your heart, and with reflection."

[My Daughter in Jesus Christ,]

I am replying to you a bit late, but still as soon as it has been possible. I am very glad that you shared the burden of your heart in your letter. Certainly, it is not small, but be at peace: thus far, you have done nothing wrong before God; on the contrary, you have acted very well. It is clear that the good God inspired you to act in the way you should, and he has assisted you in a special way. You should, then, give special thanks to him for this.

Nonetheless, for your greater assurance, I will describe for you a way of dealing with this situation that you can follow and that will give you the greatest peace in it.

First, try to be as humble as you can because this is God's intention in permitting you to undergo this kind of trial. Be very humble before God because, in this way, God will pour out upon you in abundance all the graces you need. Enter often into yourself; see the pride that reigns there and the other unworthy passions from which you cannot free yourself by your own strength. Recognize what you are of yourself, confess that you are weakness itself, then turn to the infinite goodness of God and cry out without ceasing, "*Abyssus miseriarum invocat abyssum misericordiarum*" [The abyss of misery invokes the abyss of mercy].

Second, live always in the presence of God. Try to remember this presence above all when things are most difficult. Reflect that the good God is close to you, that he desires to see how you will respond in this time of tribulation. Reflect further that his presence is not fruitless and barren but that he gives you spiritual weapons, that is, his holy grace, which he always lavishes with great abundance and which is infinitely more powerful that any difficulty you may face. Consider, too, that he cares deeply that you overcome in these trials because he is always a Father, a Friend, and a most loving, tender, and caring Spouse, who stands before you and at your side. Raise your heart to him often in sweet conversation, addressing him with humble and insistent prayers, at times seeking his help, at times expressing your confidence in him or your love for him. Say to him, for example, "Our help is in the name of the Lord" [Ps. 124:8], "In you, Lord, I take refuge; let me never be put to shame" [Ps. 31:2], "I love you, Lord, my strength, my fortress, my deliverer" [see Ps. 18:2–3], and similar prayers.

## If You Want Peace in This Life

Third, take great care never to let it show outwardly when you are troubled by this. Do not even allow such trouble into your own spirit and your heart. Guard yourself, too, from bad moods in your relations with others; be gentle toward yourself and toward them. Strive for such gentleness in bearing this trial with patience, and do not condemn yourself so easily of sin, knowing that any sin, in order to be such, must be freely chosen and carried out with deliberation and knowledge, and this will never be the case for you as long as you abhor such things. As long as you remain humble and keep yourself in God's presence, as I have just said, never let anything trouble the peace of your heart, but follow Jesus' teaching when he says, "By your perseverance you will secure your lives" [Luke 21:19].[28] Take care not to be discouraged. Saint Francis de Sales says: death, rather than to lose courage. Put your hope in God, and in his own time, he will set you free. Be gentle toward your neighbor because it is then that one is most tempted to bad moods and to impatience. Remember often what the Savior said, "Blessed are the meek, for they will inherit the land" [Matt. 5:5]; that is, blessed are they who are gentle toward themselves and others in the way I have just said, for to them it is given to control their passions.

But you will say to me: How should I act in regard to this person? I reply, avoid him and never speak to him without real cause. This is, I believe,

*"In His Own Time He Will Set You Free"*

the heart of your letter. We will speak of this at greater length when I have the opportunity to see you in a few days, and if you continue to be troubled, you will let me know.

[With all possible desire for your spiritual progress, I am,

Your father in Jesus Christ,<br>Father Bruno Lanteri]

Take time now to reflect and pray with the following:

1. "Try to be as humble as you can because this is God's intention in permitting you to undergo this kind of trial. Be very humble before God because, in this way, God will pour out upon you in abundance all the graces you need."

Be humble, like Mary, who "rejoices in God my savior, for he has looked upon his handmaid's lowliness" (see Luke 1:47–48).

Like Saint Thérèse, who writes to her sister and godmother, Marie, "Dear Sister, how can you say after this that my desires are the sign of my love?... Ah! I really feel that it is not this at all that pleases God in my little soul; what pleases Him is that *He sees me loving my littleness* and my *poverty, the blind hope that I have in His mercy*.... That is my only treasure, dear Godmother, why would this treasure not be yours?"[29]

"In this way, God will pour out upon you in abundance all the graces you need."

2. "Recognize what you are of yourself, confess that you are weakness itself, then turn to the infinite goodness of God and cry out without ceasing, '*Abyssus miseriarum invocat abyssum misericordiarum*' [The abyss of misery invokes the abyss of mercy]."

> Yes, call out, cry out, now, again, and once more, "From the depth of my limitations, my struggles, my burden, I call out with great confidence to the infinite depths of your love, your mercy, your compassion."

3. "Live always in the presence of God. Try to remember this presence above all when things are most difficult. Reflect that the good God is close to you, that he desires to see how you will respond in this time of tribulation."

> Saint Augustine: "You are more intimate to me than I am to myself."[30] More intimate to me than I am to myself. Stop here. Think about this truth.
>
> "Try to remember this presence above all when things are most difficult."

4. "Say to him, for example, 'Our help is in the name of the LORD,' 'In you, LORD, I take refuge; let me never be put to shame,' 'I love you, LORD, my strength, my fortress, my deliverer,' and similar prayers."

> Say this to him now. Say it slowly; say it from your heart, "Our help is …," "In you, LORD …," "I love you, LORD …" Say any similar prayers that you love.

## "In His Own Time He Will Set You Free"

5. "As long as you remain humble and keep yourself in God's presence, as I have just said, never let anything trouble the peace of your heart, but follow Jesus' teaching when he says, 'By your perseverance you will secure your lives.'"

Remain humble, with the joyful humility of Mary. Remain in God's presence, he who is more intimate to you than you are to yourself. And then, never let anything trouble the peace of your heart.

## 14

## "An Ounce of Prayer Made with Patience"

Sister Crocifissa Bracchetto was another religious expelled from her monastery when the French Revolution swept through Turin. Like Sister Leopolda, she was compelled to manage as best she could, and like her, she turned to Venerable Bruno for assistance. After the fall of Napoleon, he helped her to reenter religious life. The transition to a new community was not entirely easy for her, and through these vicissitudes, the letters of Venerable Bruno were her support.

Several of her letters to Venerable Bruno have been conserved, but none of his to her. An ample selection, however, of quotations from Venerable Bruno's letters to her has remained. The letters quoted range over twenty years and witness to an ongoing correspondence. The handwriting of these selections is that of Father Loggero, Venerable Bruno's assistant. Father Loggero may have selected and copied these quotations during the retreats he gave Sister Crocifissa's community.

# If You Want Peace in This Life

From the quotations, I have gathered those belonging to the letter Venerable Bruno wrote to Sister Crocifissa on December 8, 1815. Hence the absence of his usual personal tone in the beginning and end of the letter, and also the patchwork quality of the text.

Read, now, Venerable Bruno's letter. Read "with lively faith, hope, and love ... stopping for a moment where the words speak to you, with desire, with pauses, with the affection of your heart, and with reflection."

[Dearest Daughter in Jesus Christ,]

We must expect ups and downs in our practices of prayer—that is, that it will cost us something at times when we undertake them. God permits this to keep us humble and to give us more abundant graces. All this is for our spiritual progress.

For your meditation, begin it with desire and love. Never omit or shorten it because you find it burdensome or because distractions weigh upon you.

An ounce of prayer made with patience is worth more than a hundred pounds of prayer when you feel fervent, because of the heroic acts we practice in the former and because of the danger of vanity in the second. This is a teaching of Saint Francis de Sales.

Your meditation will help you as a preparation for Holy Communion and for your thanksgiving after you receive it.

With regard to discouragement, never let yourself be troubled, regardless of the state in which you find yourself, as when you feel that your faith is weak, when you feel indifferent to spiritual things, have no feeling as you do them, feel resistances, or any other defect or failing. Rather, with simplicity and with a humble heart before God, tell him with courage that you want to be his own, just as you are, and perhaps even more imperfect than you know yourself to be. Be sure in your heart that he came from Heaven precisely for sinners and that, according to his promise, his help and grace will be abundant where sin abounds [Rom. 5:20]. To allow your heart to dwell in melancholy and discouragement is to follow the spirit of the tempter. The Spirit of God leads us to confidence and peace of heart.

When you experience temptations, you need not make an exterior sign in order to reject them. An act of love of God or of rejection of the temptation is enough. Disregard, also, even the *doubt* as to whether you have been diligent in rejecting the temptations. Even if there were some negligence or failure in this regard, an act of love of God resolves everything with no need for such searching examinations and trouble of heart.

When you have failed, and you are in doubt as to whether the failure was serious or not, decide without hesitation in your own favor because such doubt is incompatible with complete awareness and full consent. When you fail, say, "It was good for me that you humbled me" [Ps. 119:71], and remember that God permits these failings for our profit and our more solid progress.

In such failings, do not be troubled or hard on yourself. Rather, let your hope be the more lively, saying, "Why are you cast down?... Hope in the LORD" [Ps. 43:5, RSVCE].

> [Your devoted servant and
> affectionate father in Jesus Christ,
> Father Bruno Lanteri]

Take time now to reflect and pray with the following:

1. "We must expect ups and downs in our practices of prayer—that is, that it will cost us something at times when we undertake them. God permits this to keep us humble and to give us more abundant graces. All this is for our spiritual progress."

You experience easier and more difficult times in your prayer. All this is within God's loving providence:

## "An Ounce of Prayer Made with Patience"

"God permits this to keep us humble and to give us more abundant graces."

"God . . . gives grace to the humble" (James 4:6).

"All this is for our spiritual progress." Reflect on this. Speak to the Lord about it.

2. "An ounce of prayer made with patience is worth more than a hundred pounds of prayer when you feel fervent, because of the heroic acts we practice in the former and because of the danger of vanity in the second. This is a teaching of Saint Francis de Sales."

"An ounce of prayer made with patience," when it is not easy, when we might omit or shorten it, and we do not. There is a heroism, there are "heroic acts," in such prayer, and it is beautiful in the eyes of God.

3. "To allow your heart to dwell in melancholy and discouragement is to follow the spirit of the tempter. The Spirit of God leads us to confidence and peace of heart."

The tempter, says Saint Ignatius of Loyola, "bites, saddens, places obstacles, and disquiets with false reasons." God gives "courage and strength, consolations, tears, inspirations, and eases and takes away all obstacles."[31]

Turn your heart away from the first; open it to the second, to God. Ask for this grace.

4. "When you fail, say, 'It was good for me that you humbled me,' and remember that God permits these failings for our profit and our more solid progress."

Can you say this when you fail? Can you try? Can you ask God for this grace? God permits this only "for our profit and our more solid progress."

5. "In such failings, do not be troubled or hard on yourself. Rather, let your hope be the more lively, saying, "Why are you cast down?... Hope in the Lord."

You have failed in this or that area. Do not be troubled. Do not be hard on yourself. Rather, have the greater trust in God. Say, "Why are you downcast, my soul? Why do you groan within me? Wait for God, for I shall again praise him, my savior and my God" (Ps. 43:5).

## 15

## "If You Want Peace in This Life"

Venerable Bruno writes a letter of spiritual direction to a wife and mother, Clementina Celebrini, in reply to her letter. Clementina was instrumental in arranging for the Oblates who would preach a widely attended parish mission in the Cathedral of Fossano, her home city, a fact that attests to her life of faith and her activity on behalf of it. Venerable Bruno encourages her to accept the trials that God permits, to avoid turning in on herself, and to lift her heart often to God.

Read, now, Venerable Bruno's letter. Read "with lively faith, hope, and love ... stopping for a moment where the words speak to you, with desire, with pauses, with the affection of your heart, and with reflection."

# If You Want Peace in This Life

Madame,

Forgive me that I have not replied earlier to your letter, as I could not. I have done what you asked, and you need not be anxious. You would like to live already in Heaven, where happy events are not followed by trials, but you must be patient because you must still remain here on earth and must suffer with patience the trials necessary to enter Heaven.

If you want peace in this life, you must, first of all, decide to accommodate yourself to circumstances and not demand that circumstances accommodate themselves to you. You must, secondly, seek to practice uniformity of your will with God's. It is he who disposes everything, arranges everything, and permits all that takes place. We need only seek and follow his fatherly design, which is always to provide us with opportunities for practicing different virtues, at times one, at times another, so that he will have something for which to reward us.

I have noticed in your letters that you often turn in on yourself. Try to watch out for this and to focus less often on yourself but to serve God with great simplicity. Instead of turning in on yourself, lift your gaze often with peace and love to God, to his lovable will, to his adorable providence. Tell him that, regardless of whether you are good or bad, you

## "If You Want Peace in This Life"

want to be totally his and that it is his to make you become better. Cast also upon him all your concerns about your children and your husband. The more you trust in him, the greater will be his care for you. Pray for me. I bless you, and I leave you in the Sacred Heart of Jesus.

> Your humble servant and father in Jesus Christ,
> Father Bruno Lanteri

Take time now to reflect and pray with the following:

1. "You would like to live already in Heaven, where happy events are not followed by trials, but you must be patient because you must still remain here on earth and must suffer with patience the trials necessary to enter Heaven."

"I waited patiently for the LORD; he inclined to me and heard my cry" (Ps. 40:1, RSVCE).

"Rejoice in your hope, be patient in tribulation, be constant in prayer" (Rom. 12:12, RSVCE).

"Love is patient" (1 Cor. 13:4).

"You must be patient because you must still remain here on earth and must suffer with patience the trials necessary to enter Heaven." Ask for this grace.

2. "If you want peace in this life, you must, first of all, decide to accommodate yourself to circumstances and not demand that circumstances accommodate themselves to you.

## If You Want Peace in This Life

You must, secondly, seek to practice uniformity of your will with God's."

You want peace in your life. Venerable Bruno shows us the path to such peace: to "decide to accommodate yourself to circumstances" and to "practice uniformity of your will with God's." Circumstances: the place where you live, your family, your work, other relationships, finances, home, health …

Two things that bring peace: "decide to accommodate yourself … seek to practice uniformity." Ask for this double grace.

3. "We need only seek and follow his fatherly design, which is always to provide us opportunities for practicing different virtues, at times one, at times another, so that he will have something for which to reward us."

This is our call in the circumstances of our lives, to "seek and follow his fatherly design," his loving providence in our lives.

His loving providence: "Are not two sparrows sold for a small coin? Yet not one of them falls to the ground without your Father's knowledge. Even all the hairs of your head are counted" (Matt. 10:29–30).

He provides "opportunities for practicing different virtues," with a view to our eternal reward.

4. "I have noticed in your letters that you often turn in on yourself. Try to watch out for this and to focus less often on yourself but to serve God with great simplicity. Instead

*"If You Want Peace in This Life"*

of turning in on yourself, lift your gaze often with peace and love to God, to his lovable will, to his adorable providence."

Turning inward in sadness and loneliness. Turning outward toward God in relationship and hope. Avoid the first. Embrace the second.

"Lift your gaze often with peace and love to God, to his lovable will, to his adorable providence." Often. With peace and love.

5. "Cast also upon him all your concerns about your children and your husband. The more you trust in him, the greater will be his care for you."

Concerns about your family, about your husband or wife, about your children, any other concerns in your life: "Cast all your worries upon him because he cares for you" (1 Pet. 5:7).

Father Loggero writes of Venerable Bruno, "He took this saying deeply to heart and it was never far from his thoughts: 'The one who hopes for everything, obtains everything.'"[32]

16

# "This Will Be the Remedy for Any Sadness"

Gabriella Solaro della Margarita was no stranger to tragedy. Her first marriage ended abruptly with the premature death of her husband. No children were born of this marriage. In her second marriage, Gabriella had six children—four boys and two girls. Three of the boys died young. The remaining boy, Clemente, would become well known in later years as a government official, noteworthy also for his public practice and support of the Catholic Faith, a stance seldom seen in such circles at the time. In all likelihood, Venerable Bruno was his spiritual director. Of the two girls, one married, and the other entered religious life.

When the armies of the French Revolution invaded the region, the family home was devastated, and the family had to flee for their lives. The raising of her children was no easy task for Gabriella in such times. She was a strong woman, decisive, and a leader—she had to be in such circumstances—a

## If You Want Peace in This Life

faithful Catholic, but also somewhat sharp and impatient. When he writes, Venerable Bruno calls her to growth in this area.

In the letter given here, Venerable Bruno has just learned from Gabriella's mother-in-law that Gabriella's little son Enrico has died. We can only imagine what this death meant for Gabriella, already burdened by the death of a husband and two sons. Venerable Bruno, knowing this, immediately writes to her.

A woman who had lost a son at eighteen in tragic circumstances read this letter and said, "This is the most consoling thing I have ever read since the death of my son." She is not alone in that response. That Gabriella always kept this letter indicates her similar regard for it.

As always, Venerable Bruno begins with the human, with the heart. He validates and shares Gabriella's great sorrow. But he does not remain there. He then turns to the level of faith and invites Gabriella to live her loss above all on this level, the level of its deepest and most consoling truth.

In this letter, Venerable Bruno speaks to all who have lost loved ones.

Read, now, Venerable Bruno's letter. Read "with lively faith, hope, and love ... stopping for a moment where the words speak to you, with desire, with pauses, with the affection of your heart, and with reflection."

# "This Will Be the Remedy for Any Sadness"

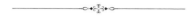

July 31, 1818

Madame,

When I learned from your mother-in-law that you had lost your little Enrico, I felt great sorrow for what you must be undergoing because no sacrifice could be more painful for you. He had such wonderful qualities that all loved him, and how much more the love of his mother. And so, because of this, you have every reason to feel his loss and to weep for him.

Yet, in another way, I share with you a joy that you have surely gained a protector in Heaven who cannot fail to care for you because he is your son. And because you love him so deeply, turn your thoughts to his eternal happiness, share in his glory, and do not imagine that you have lost him. It would be wrong to think so because you have lost him only from sight and not in reality.

Consider that he is at your side like another angel, that he encourages you to dedicate yourself to the things of Heaven and to share in his joy; that he assures you of his efforts before the throne of the Most Holy Trinity for you, for his father, his brother, and his dear sisters, to obtain for all of you great and abundant graces for your eternal salvation.

## If You Want Peace in This Life

Remain in continual and loving conversation with him. Speak to him about all that you experience in your own heart, all that happens in your family, and anything of importance for you. Be on guard against thinking that he does not care about you or that he is powerless to help you. That would be to misunderstand the immense love and almost infinite power that each of the Blessed enjoys, with all the other divine perfections that God shares with them in the greatest possible abundance.

And so, if before you had no reason to be discouraged in the service of God, you have much less reason now. I would add that if it were possible for your little Enrico to feel any sorrow even now in Heaven, it would be to see you discouraged and saddened because of him, because of your own failings, or because of the difficulties you encounter in the service of God. This will be the remedy for any sadness or lack of courage you may feel: the thought that, with the grace of God and the protection of your little Enrico, you can do all things.

I beg you to share some of these reflections with your respected and worthy daughters to console them also in their great affliction for the loss of their beloved brother. Tell them that I, too, share in their pain and that I will hold them constantly present in the Holy Sacrifice of the Mass to obtain

## "This Will Be the Remedy for Any Sadness"

for them consolation of heart and their spiritual growth.

I end this letter by blessing you all, and I am, with all possible esteem and respect,

> Your servant and father in Jesus Christ,
> Father Bruno Lanteri

---

Take time now to reflect and pray with the following:

1. "I felt great sorrow for what you must be undergoing because no sacrifice could be more painful for you. He had such wonderful qualities that all loved him, and how much more the love of his mother. And so, because of this, you have every reason to feel his loss and to weep for him."

"And Jesus wept" (John 11:35). At the death of his friend Lazarus, Jesus wept. He knows and reverences human sorrow and tears at the loss of a loved one.

Venerable Bruno, who experienced the early death of his parents and the death of all nine of his brothers and sisters, knows this too: "I felt great sorrow for what you must be undergoing."

Let Jesus reverence your human sorrow.

2. "Yet, in another way, I share with you a joy that you have surely gained a protector in Heaven who cannot fail to care for you because he is your son. And because you love him so deeply, turn your thoughts to his eternal happiness,

share in his glory, and do not imagine that you have lost him. It would be wrong to think so because you have lost him only from sight and not in reality."

> Now, with Venerable Bruno, with Gabriella, open your heart to the truth of faith: "in another way, I share with you a joy that you have surely gained a protector in Heaven who cannot fail to care for you." Consider this in terms of a loved one whom you have lost. "Turn your thoughts to his [or her] eternal happiness."
>
> "Do not imagine that you have lost him [or her]." Yes, turn your thoughts to your deceased loved one. Do not imagine that you have lost him (or her).

3. "Consider that he is at your side like another angel, that he encourages you to dedicate yourself to the things of Heaven, and to share in his joy; that he assures you of his efforts before the throne of the Most Holy Trinity for you."

> Yes, consider this. "He [or she] is at your side like another angel."
>
> "He [or she] encourages you to dedicate yourself to the things of Heaven."
>
> "Share in his [or her] joy."
>
> "He [or she] assures you of his [of her] efforts before the throne of the Most Holy Trinity for you."
>
> Consider all this.

4. "Be on guard against thinking that he does not care about you or that he is powerless to help you. That would

## "This Will Be the Remedy for Any Sadness"

be to misunderstand the immense love and almost infinite power that each of the Blessed enjoys, with all the other divine perfections that God shares with them in the greatest possible abundance."

> Know that your deceased loved one cares for you, is powerful before God to help you. Think of "the immense love and almost infinite power that each of the Blessed enjoys." Your dear one's love for you is greater than ever. By God's gift, he or she has "almost infinite power to help you."
>
> Turn to him, to her. Be glad to know of that immense love for you. Ask for that powerful intercession.

5. "And so, if before you had no reason to be discouraged in the service of God, you have much less reason now.... This will be the remedy for any sadness or lack of courage you may feel: the thought that, with the grace of God and the protection of your little Enrico, you can do all things."

> "This will be the remedy." This thought, "that, with the grace of God and the protection of your loved one with the Lord, you can do all things."

# 17

## "Careful Never to Belittle Yourself"

Venerable Bruno offers counsels to a religious whose life in community is not easy. In the unfinished draft conserved, she is not named.[33] She fears that in responding poorly to these struggles, she is failing the Lord. Venerable Bruno, as so often, shows her that even should she fail, by responding well to her failure, she will grow spiritually. He calls her—and us, in our relational struggles—out of discouragement and into hope.

Read, now, Venerable Bruno's letter. Read "with lively faith, hope, and love … stopping for a moment where the words speak to you, with desire, with pauses, with the affection of your heart, and with reflection."

# If You Want Peace in This Life

―――――――――◦•❖•◦―――――――――

March 26, 1820

Dearest Daughter in Jesus Christ,

I have always believed that those shops that do much business are the best. I have to say, then, that this monastery where you have many occasions to grow spiritually richer is the best "shop" you could have chosen.

But you want to say to me that instead of growing richer in merit, you only increase in demerit. To this I reply that either you practice virtue in these occasions and so grow in merit, or you fall into some defect, in which case you have the opportunity for greater merit: first, in humility, as you grow in concrete self-knowledge; second, in hope, as you turn with confidence to your heavenly Father and say to him, "*Dimitte nobis*" ["Forgive us," from the Our Father]; third, in love of God to remedy in this way the coldness shown him in his divine service. It will be all the easier to gain these merits with the acts just mentioned if you are careful never to belittle yourself, nor to marvel at these ongoing defects, but rather to say with peace, at every moment, "It was good for me that you humbled me" [Ps. 119:71] and "*Nunc coepi*" [Now I begin].

Neither be afraid that these occasions you lament should be avoided, because you know that they are

## "Careful Never to Belittle Yourself"

rather to be sought, and if you read *The Spiritual Combat*, you will be confirmed in this understanding.

> [Your servant and father in Jesus Christ,
> Father Bruno Lanteri]

---

Take time now to reflect and pray with the following:

1. "I have always believed that those shops that do much business are the best. I have to say, then, that this monastery where you have many occasions to grow spiritually richer is the best 'shop' you could have chosen."

Blessed Solanus Casey: "Do not pray for easy lives, pray to be stronger. Do not pray for tasks equal to your powers, pray for powers equal to your tasks. Then the doing of your work shall be no miracle, but you shall be a miracle. Every day you shall wonder at yourself, at the richness of life that has come to you by the grace of God."[34]

2. "But you want to say to me that instead of growing richer in merit, you only increase in demerit. To this I reply that either you practice virtue in these occasions and so grow in merit, or you fall into some defect, in which case you have the opportunity for greater merit."

There is no place for discouragement in the times of our failings. Not even in the times of our failings. Ponder this.

3. "You have the opportunity for greater merit: first, in humility, as you grow in concrete self-knowledge; second, in hope, as you turn with confidence to your heavenly Father and say to him, '*Dimitte nobis*' ["Forgive us," from the Our Father]; third, in love of God to remedy in this way the coldness shown him in his divine service."

Greater merit when you fall into some defect: an opportunity to be humble—"God … bestows favor on the humble" (1 Pet. 5:5)—to turn with confidence to our loving Father and ask forgiveness, and to express love for him.

4. "It will be all the easier to gain these merits with the acts just mentioned if you are careful never to belittle yourself, nor marvel at these ongoing defects, but rather to say with peace, at every moment, 'It was good for me that you humbled me.'"

"Be careful never to belittle yourself." Never belittle yourself. Never.

"Nor marvel at these ongoing defects." Rather, "say with peace," "at every moment," "It was good for me that you humbled me," because of the greater merit this makes possible.

Say this. Say it with peace.

*"Careful Never to Belittle Yourself"*

5. "Say with peace, at every moment ... '*Nunc coepi*' [Now I begin]."

Saint Paul VI: "I will no longer look back, but do willingly, simply, humbly, and courageously, the duty arising from the circumstances in which I find myself, understanding it as your will. To do it quickly. To do everything. To do it well. To do joyfully that which you want of me right now."[35] Quickly. Everything. Well. Joyfully. Ask for this grace.

18

## "Paradise Pays for Everything"

The following is a draft of the final letter conserved from Venerable Bruno to Leopoldo Ricasoli. Venerable Bruno writes from Rome, where he has just obtained papal approval of the Oblates of the Virgin Mary. He had planned to visit with Leopoldo in Florence on his journey north from Rome, but months of absence from his many obligations in Turin, delays in Rome that required him to postpone his trip again and again, and his worsening health no longer permitted this.

The sacrifice is great, as both he and Leopoldo know they will most likely never meet again. Venerable Bruno writes, "We shall both have to make this sacrifice to God, which I confess is not small for me." He quotes a saying of his mentor and spiritual director, Father Nikolaus Diessbach, himself no stranger to suffering, that "il paradiso paga tutto," "paradise pays for everything."

## If You Want Peace in This Life

Leopoldo has offered the Oblates a property of his outside Florence. Grateful for the offer, Venerable Bruno tells him that they cannot yet expand this far from Turin.

Leopoldo's son, a Jesuit novice and the future Father Luigi Ricasoli, S.J., resides at the Jesuit novitiate in Rome. During his stay there, Venerable Bruno tried several times to meet him but was never able to do so.

Venerable Bruno and Leopoldo would meet when Venerable Bruno traveled north from Rome, though only for some hours, in Poggibonsi, a small city thirty miles south of Florence. Of this meeting, Leopoldo writes, "I thank God that I saw you, and this was a true miracle."[36] In all probability, it was their final meeting.

Read, now, Venerable Bruno's letter. Read "with lively faith, hope, and love ... stopping for a moment where the words speak to you, with desire, with pauses, with the affection of your heart, and with reflection."

[Monsieur and dear Friend in Jesus Christ,]

I have waited until now to reply to your gracious letter, hoping every day to be able to let you know the time of my departure, and so of my consolation in the thought of seeing you again, but it was in vain. Only now have I finalized my task [approval of the Oblates], but I still have to remain here some days

## "Paradise Pays for Everything"

more to receive some important papers, and this long delay, together with my health problems, which increase constantly, forces me to hasten my return as much as possible, so that, to my great regret, I will no longer be able to stop in Florence. We shall both have to make this sacrifice to God, which I confess is not small for me.

I thank you for the offer of your country residence for our Congregation, but we are not able at present to accept it because the number of members is small, and for some years yet we will not be able to expand outside of Piedmont.

I will also leave Rome regretting that I was not able to meet your son, the Jesuit novice. I went a number of times to the novitiate but was never able to see him. I could not go there more often because my lodgings were so far away and because of issues of health.

Once again, this life is destined for continual sacrifices to the Lord, and Father Diessbach used to say that Paradise pays for everything. I beg you always to keep me especially present in your devout prayers, and with sentiments of the highest esteem, respect, and gratitude, I am,

> [Your Servant and Christian Friend,
> Father Bruno Lanteri
> September 1826]

## If You Want Peace in This Life

Take time now to reflect and pray with the following:

> "Once again this life is destined for continual sacrifices to the Lord, and Father Diessbach used to say that Paradise pays for everything." "Paradise pays for everything." Pause to reflect on this. All the more when your life seems "destined for continual sacrifice."
>
> Spend a short time reflecting on each of the following. Let thought become conversation with God.

1. "I consider that the sufferings of this present time are as nothing compared with the glory to be revealed for us" (Rom. 8:18).

2. "He will wipe every tear from their eyes, and there shall be no more death or mourning, wailing or pain, [for] the old order has passed away" (Rev. 21:4).

3. "If then you were raised with Christ, seek what is above, where Christ is seated at the right hand of God. Think of what is above, not of what is on earth" (Col. 3:1-2).

4. "Paradise pays for everything." Everything.

5. Saint Thérèse to Céline Maudelonde, a childhood playmate, both now twenty-one, Thérèse in religious life, Céline married: "They have passed away, then, for us both the blessed days of our childhood! We are now at the serious stage of life; the road we are following is different, however, the goal is the same. Both of us must have only one same purpose: to *sanctify* ourselves in the way God has traced out for us."[37]

# 19

## "His Whole Being Was at Peace"

The following letters are written by a layman whom Venerable Bruno directed in a retreat.[38] They present Venerable Bruno the year before his death, already in weak physical condition. These were the final months of a life marked by constant struggles with poor health.

Michele di Cavour, father of renowned Italian statesman Camillo di Cavour, entered the Oblate house in Pinerolo to make an eight-day retreat. He was one of thirty-six laymen lodged in the house during these days. Other external retreatants, men and women, joined them in the church for the talks given by the Oblate priests. During the retreat, Michele wrote twice to his wife, Adèle, and in these letters commented on his meetings with Venerable Bruno.

Michele's mention of Venerable Bruno's spiritual assistance to his grandmother indicates a preexisting relationship. The Vaudier mentioned was most likely a family place of vacation. Superga is a large hill on the outskirts of Turin, Michele's

## If You Want Peace in This Life

place of residence. He speaks of ten days of retreat—that is, eight full days that began the evening before the first full day and ended the morning after the final full day.

The memory of those days of grace did not fade for Michele. In a letter written to Venerable Bruno the following month, he thanked him "for all the goodness you showed me when I made the Exercises," and in another letter, he added, "The memory of those days spent in solitude remains with me. I owe to those days much of the peace I feel, and I hope to be able to renew the experience again."[39]

The following are excerpts from the two letters to his wife.

Read, now, these letters. Read "with lively faith, hope, and love ... stopping for a moment where the words speak to you, with desire, with pauses, with the affection of your heart, and with reflection."

*First letter, second day, 5:30 a.m.*

My room looks out on the side of Superga, and, at this hour, after having thought about God, I think of you. This life of retreat seems to suit me in everything. In the first place, by inclination I prefer to obey rather than command; here, the obedience is to a man who is most gentle [Venerable Bruno]. The body receives all it needs; I feel better here than at Vaudier, and I sense that the time here will do me more good than that spent in Vaudier. There is also physical exercise, since we go to the church ten times during the day; ten times, therefore, that I think more especially of all of you.

The superior, Father Lanteri, is very gentle. His health could not be worse, but I prefer to speak with him because he assisted Grandmother, whose final moments are constantly present to my memory. My room is next to his, and I talk with him during the two hours of recreation after lunch and after supper. The rest of the time we are in silence, and I continue to welcome it.

Goodbye, my tender Adèle, my good mother, my dear Franquin, and my children. I will pray for you and will contribute to your happiness by gaining interior peace. I embrace you all.

*Second letter, begun on day four*
I received your letter. It is the rule that during these ten days we should suspend all correspondence foreign to the great work with which we are to occupy ourselves. For that very reason, the superiors permit letters that, rather than distract from that purpose, reinforce, fortify, and encourage it. I have not replied to you with my pen because I had more important occupations; but I have replied to you with my heart, because God does not forbid that I join to the idea of drawing close to him that of being united with you in an eternity

of glorifying, blessing, and thanking him for having created us.

For myself, I can tell you that I am very happy with the Abbé Lanteri. I have spent much time with him. I find him gentle, persuasive, and, above all, most considerate. God gives him much light to understand and explain things very well.

*Conclusion to the second letter,*
*written on day five, 9:00 a.m.*

I was deeply stirred when I received your letter. I had gone to the Abbé Lanteri to ask permission to read it. I found him physically worse than on other days. He said, "Read as much as you wish; the sentiments of the heart are pleasing to God," but tears were falling from his eyes; he could scarcely breathe. "The lamp is going out," he said. His whole being was at peace. He looks to Heaven during his attacks and pronounces the word "paradise" with so much faith that it stirs everything within me.

He did not wish to have any other penitent but me. One of the priests brought him a note from a person who asked to speak with him. Looking at me, he replied, "I have only a little breath; I am reserving it for you." The priest replied in a firm and half-severe voice: "If God has permitted that a second soul should ask for you, he has also chosen to give you enough breath to lead that soul to himself." It is

## "His Whole Being Was at Peace"

blessed, my Adèle, to shed such tears! I shed many at those words. I do not believe that the Abbé Lanteri is so close to his end.

Take time now to reflect and pray with the following:

1. "The superior, Father Lanteri, is very gentle."

"Le supèrieur, Père Lanteri, est bien doux." *Bien:* very. *Doux:* warm, gentle, considerate, compassionate, benign, kind.

Bruno's effort to acquire gentleness was lifelong and bore the fruit evidenced here.

"Learn from me, for I am gentle and lowly in heart" (Matt. 11:29, RSVCE).

Yes, learn from him, as did Venerable Bruno. Your life will bear rich fruit, and you will give peace to others.

2. "His health could not be worse."

From Venerable Bruno's biography: "He was a man of shattered health, often utterly unable to work, exhausted by an oppression of the chest, at times scarcely able to breathe, and constantly aware that physical effort might cause a recurrence of these attacks. His eyes were ruined, and frequently he was unable to read."[40]

Blessed Jan Roothaan writes of Venerable Bruno at age sixty-five, after describing him as physically "very weak": "In these days I have heard that he was able to accomplish, for the glory of God, a thing that, in view of his condition and the brief time in which he did it, may rightly seem a miracle."[41]

From a letter of Venerable Bruno to a woman in poor health: "Show yourself joyful even when you do not feel so because of physical problems. At such times more than ever, guard against closing in on yourself, and turn your thought to Paradise, because it is yours."[42] Yes, show yourself joyful even in such times. Ask for at least some of this grace.

3. "God gives him much light to understand and explain things very well."

In the communion of saints, bring now your doubts, your questions, your need for clarity to Venerable Bruno. Ask him to bring you the light you need, as he did for so many during his life.

4. "Read as much as you wish; the sentiments of the heart are pleasing to God."

Is there someone close to you or even at a physical distance who is waiting for a word of encouragement, of presence, of support, of understanding from you? Speak that word to that person; write that word to that person. Share those sentiments that are pleasing to God and will be heartening for that person.

5. "Tears were falling from his eyes; he could scarcely breathe. 'The lamp is going out,' he said. His whole being

## "His Whole Being Was at Peace"

was at peace. He looks to Heaven during his attacks and pronounces the word 'paradise' with so much faith that it stirs everything within me."

Reread these words. Slowly. Imagine this scene. Be there. Ask for a similar love for Heaven, a similar faith, a similar peace.

# Prayer for the Intercession of Venerable Bruno Lanteri

O Father, fountain of all life and holiness,
You gave Venerable Bruno Lanteri great faith in Christ, your Son, a lively hope, and an active love for the salvation of his brethren.
You made him a prophet of your word and a witness to your mercy.
He had a tender love for Mary, and by his very life he taught fidelity to the Church.
Father, hear the prayer of your family, and, through the intercession of Venerable Bruno, grant us the grace for which we now ask …
May he be raised to the altars that we may give you greater praise. We ask this through your Son, Jesus Christ, our Lord. Amen.

For information about Venerable Bruno Lanteri's cause of canonization, to ask for prayers, or to relate graces received through his intercession, visit https://www.omvusa.org/bruno-lanteri/.

For a documentary on Venerable Bruno Lanteri, see: https://www.omvusa.org/bruno-lanteri/life-legacy/documentary/.

For young men interested in joining the Oblates of the Virgin Mary, visit https://www.omvusa.org/becoming-an-oblate/.

# Endnotes

1 Timothy Gallagher, O.M.V., *Begin Again: The Life and Spiritual Legacy of Bruno Lanteri* (New York: Crossroad Publishing, 2013), 8.
2 Gallagher, *Begin Again*, 6-7.
3 In some cases, I have also simplified the elaborate initial salutations and closings with the extended personal titles that were customary at the time and might be distracting to today's reader. In his letters, Venerable Bruno signs himself in varied ways, according to different settings: in official letters, as "Theologian," the title of one with a doctorate in theology; at times, simply with his name; at other times, more rapidly with his initials alone; and in the drafts, with no signature at all. When the letters are in French, he is titled "L'Abbé Lanteri." I have rendered all these, according to today's usage, as "Father Bruno Lanteri."
4 Timothy Gallagher, O.M.V., ed., *Un'esperienza dello Spirito: Pio Bruno Lanteri: Il suo carisma nelle sue parole* (Cuneo: AGA, 1989), 73.

5 Tob. 12:14 in some versions.
6 In all likelihood, these are chapters 9 and 10 of part 4 of Saint Francis de Sales's *Introduction to the Devout Life*, "How to Remedy Minor Temptations" and "How It Is Necessary to Fortify the Heart against Temptations."
7 Paolo Calliari, O.M.V., ed., *Carteggio del Venerabile Padre Pio Bruno Lanteri (1759–1830), fondatore della Congregazione degli Oblati di Maria Vergine* (Turin: Editrice Lanteriana, 1976), 4:201–202.
8 It was founded by Venerable Bruno's long-time spiritual director and mentor, Father Nikolaus Diessbach, and sought to use the printed word—the chief means of communication of ideas in that day—on behalf of the Faith. See Gallagher, *Begin Again*, 22–29.
9 Soeur Geneviève de la Sainte-Face [Céline Martin], *Thérèse de Lisieux: Conseils et Souvenirs* (Paris: Éditions du Cerf, 1973), 72. Author's translation.
10 Calliari, *Carteggio*, 2:342–343.
11 "*La paciencia todo lo alcanza*," her classic "Bookmark."
12 *Pio Bruno Lanteri: Scritti e documenti d'archivio* (Rome: Edizioni Lanteri, 2002), 1, 759.
13 General Audience, September 16, 2009, https://www.vatican.va/content/benedict-xvi/en/audiences/2009/documents/hf_ben-xvi_aud_20090916.html.
14 Joyce Emert, *Louis Martin: The Father of a Saint* (New York: Alba House, 1983), 58.
15 Calliari, *Carteggio*, 4:211.
16 *Spiritual Exercises*, para. 23. Author's translation.
17 *St. Thérèse of Lisieux: Her Last Conversations*, trans. John Clarke, O.C.D. (Washington, D.C.: ICS Publications, 1977), 251.
18 Marion A. Habig, ed., *St. Francis of Assisi: Writings and Early Biographies* (Quincy, IL: Franciscan Press, 1991), 318.

## Endnotes

19 Letter to Madame de la Fléchère, May 19, 1608, in Œuvres de Saint François De Sales, bk. 14, Letters, vol. 4, https://www.donboscosanto.eu/francesco_di_sales/Lexicon/Fontes/14-Oeuvres%20de%20Saint%20Francois%20de%20Sales-Tome%20XIV-Vol.4-Lettres.html#_Toc386401015. Author's translation.
20 The Liturgy of the Hours (New York: Catholic Book Publishing, 1975), vol. 3, 80.
21 Second Vatican Council, Dogmatic Constitution on the Church Lumen Gentium (November 21, 1964), no. 11. Author's translation.
22 John Paul II, encyclical letter Ecclesia de Eucharistia (April 17, 2003), no. 1.
23 Introduction to the Devout Life 3, 9. Author's translation.
24 Habig, St. Francis of Assisi, 655.
25 Homily, Palm Sunday, March 28, 2021, Saint Peter's Basilica.
26 The Liturgy of the Hours (New York: Catholic Book Publishing, 1975), vol. 4, 1342.
27 See Calliari, Carteggio, 2:404, where Paolo Calliari, O.M.V., who published the letter, reads it in this sense.
28 Author's translation from the Latin, which Venerable Bruno uses, according to common practice in his day.
29 Letters of St. Thérèse of Lisieux, trans. John Clarke, O.C.D. (Washington, D.C.: Institute of Carmelite Studies, 1988), vol. 2, 999.
30 Confessions 3, 6, 11. Author's translation.
31 Spiritual Exercises 315. Author's translation.
32 Amato Frutaz, ed., Pinerolien. Beatificationis et canonizationis Servi Dei Pii Brunonis Lanteri fundatoris Congregationis Oblatorum M. V. (1830): Positio super introductione causae et super virtutibus ex officio compilata (Rome: Typis Polyglottis Vaticanis, 1945), 632.

33 Paolo Calliari, O.M.V., hypothesizes that this may have been Sister Crocifissa Bracchetto. *Carteggio*, 3:264, and *Il venerabile Pio Bruno Lanteri (1759–1830) fondatore degli Oblati di Maria Vergine nella storia religiosa del suo tempo* (Typescript, 1978–1983), vol. 3, pt. 2, 260.
34 Michael Crosby, O.F.M. Cap, *Thank God Ahead of Time: The Life and Spirituality of Solanus Casey* (Cincinnati: Franciscan Media, 2009), 139.
35 Paul VI, "Pensiero alla morte," August 9, 1979, Vatican website, https://www.vatican.va/content/paul-vi/it/speeches/1978/august/documents/hf_p-vi_spe_19780806_meditazione-morte.html#*. Author's translation.
36 Calliari, *Carteggio*, 4:202.
37 *Letters of St. Thérèse of Lisieux*, vol. 2, 865.
38 Gallagher, *Begin Again*, 225–228.
39 Calliari, *Carteggio*, 5:315, 377.
40 Gallagher, *Begin Again*, 5.
41 Gallagher, *Begin Again*, 162.
42 Timothy Gallagher, O.M.V., *Overcoming Spiritual Discouragement: The Wisdom and Spiritual Power of Venerable Bruno Lanteri* (Irondale, AL: EWTN Publishing, 2019), 13.

# Bibliography

Calliari, Paolo, O.M.V., ed. *Carteggio del Venerabile Padre Pio Bruno Lanteri (1759–1830) fondatore della Congregazione degli Oblati di Maria Vergine.* 5 vols. Turin: Editrice Lanteriana, 1976.

———. *Il venerabile Pio Bruno Lanteri (1759–1830) fondatore degli Oblati di Maria Vergine nella storia religiosa del suo tempo.* Typescript, 1978–1983.

Frutaz, Amato, ed. *Pinerolien. Beatificationis et canonizationis Servi Dei Pii Brunonis Lanteri fundatoris Congregationis Oblatorum M.V. (1830): Positio super introductione causae et super virtutibus ex officio compilata.* Rome: Typis Polyglottis Vaticanis, 1945.

Gallagher, Timothy M., O.M.V. *Begin Again: The Life and Spiritual Legacy of Bruno Lanteri.* New York: Crossroad Publishing, 2013.

———. *Overcoming Spiritual Discouragement: The Wisdom and Spiritual Power of Venerable Bruno Lanteri.* Irondale, AL: EWTN Publishing, 2019.

Gallagher, Timothy, O.M.V., ed. *Un'esperienza dello Spirito. Pio Bruno Lanteri: Il suo carisma nelle sue parole.* Cuneo: AGA, 1989.

*Pio Bruno Lanteri: Scritti e documenti d'archivio.* 4 vols. Rome: Edizioni Lanteri, 2002.

# Sources of the Letters

1. Paolo Calliari, O.M.V., ed. *Carteggio del Venerabile Padre Pio Bruno Lanteri (1759-1830), fondatore della Congregazione degli Oblati di Maria Vergine*, vol. 2 (Turin: Editrice Lanteriana, 1976), 125-128.
2. *Carteggio*, 2:160-161.
3. *Carteggio*, 2:169-172.
4. *Carteggio*, 2:128-136.
5. *Carteggio*, 2:314-315.
6. *Carteggio*, 2:282.
7. *Carteggio*, 2:321-322.
8. *Carteggio*, 2:323-324.
9. *Carteggio*, 2:325-326.
10. *Carteggio*, 2:344-345.
11. *Carteggio*, 2:352.
12. *Carteggio*, 2:399-400.
13. *Carteggio*, 2:404-406.

14. *Pio Bruno Lanteri: Scritti e documenti d'archivio*, 4 vols. (Rome: Edizioni Lanteri, 2002), 1:746–761.
15. *Carteggio*, 3:164–165.
16. *Carteggio*, 3:197–199.
17. *Carteggio*, 3:264–265.
18. *Carteggio*, 4:210–211.
19. Timothy M. Gallagher, O.M.V., *Begin Again: The Life and Spiritual Legacy of Bruno Lanteri* (New York: Crossroad Publishing, 2013), 225–228.

# Resources

Timothy M. Gallagher, O.M.V., *Begin Again: The Life and Spiritual Legacy of Bruno Lanteri* (New York: Crossroad Publishing, 2013). Biography of Venerable Bruno.

Timothy M. Gallagher, O.M.V., *A Biblical Way of Praying the Mass: The Eucharistic Wisdom of Venerable Bruno Lanteri* (Irondale, AL: EWTN Publishing, 2020).

Timothy M. Gallagher, O.M.V., *Overcoming Spiritual Discouragement: The Wisdom and Spiritual Power of Venerable Bruno Lanteri* (Irondale, AL: EWTN Publishing, 2019).

Timothy M. Gallagher, O.M.V., *Overcoming Spiritual Discouragement in the Teaching of Venerable Bruno Lanteri*. Ten videorecorded talks, https://www.omvusa.org/our-work/virtual-workshops/overcoming-spiritual-discouragement/.

Timothy M. Gallagher, O.M.V., and Kris McGregor, *Begin Again: The Life of Ven. Bruno Lanteri*, eighteen-part podcast series, Discerning Hearts app and website (search under "Spiritual Formation").

Oblates of the Virgin Mary website: omvusa.org

Fr. Timothy Gallagher's website: frtimothygallagher.org

## About the Author

Father Timothy M. Gallagher, O.M.V., was ordained in 1979 as a member of the Oblates of the Virgin Mary, a religious community dedicated to giving retreats and spiritual formation according to the *Spiritual Exercises* of Saint Ignatius. Having obtained his doctorate in 1983 from the Gregorian University, he has taught (St. John's Seminary, Brighton, Massachusetts; Our Lady of Grace Seminary Residence, Boston), assisted in formation work, and served two terms as provincial in his community. He is a frequent speaker on EWTN, and his digitally recorded talks are used around the world. He has written ten books on Ignatian discernment and prayer, and several books on Venerable Bruno Lanteri and the *Liturgy of the Hours*. He currently holds the Saint Ignatius Chair for Spiritual Formation at Saint John Vianney Theological Seminary in Denver.